ELITE SCRUM

INCLUDING PREP EXAM

BY: B. REED

INCLUDING PREP EXAM

Paperback ISBN: 979-8-9916877-4-4

B. Reed., Real World Scrum: Including questions and answers to certified scrum master exam (p. 2). Ascend Management Group LLC. Kindle Edition.

Table of Contents

Origin of Scrum

R eal World Scrum has to come from somewhere. I can only take partial credit. The credit I'm willing to take is that finding a resource that will give you a boots-on-the-ground "Real World"code of conduct when working on a scrum team is hard. This book will help you understand the function and essential role of a Scrum Master and Scrum team. Some concepts will be repeated throughout this book so that I can hammer home specific topics. You will get a grasp on real-world Scrum Techniques and Tradition Scrum. Now, let's start to cook!

The Scrum framework has its roots in the 1986 paper "The New New Product Development Game" by Hirotaka Takeuchi and Ikujiro Nonaka. The authors, both Japanese business scholars, observed that traditional product development methods needed to adapt to the rapidly changing business environment. I know very little about Japan. However, Japanese businesses are as professionals as they come. Very meticulous, with close attention to detail. They proposed a new approach inspired by rugby, where teams work together, iterating and adapting quickly to achieve a common goal. Teamwork makes the API work.

In the early 1990s, Jeff Sutherland, a computer scientist, and Ken Schwaber, a software developer, began experimenting with Takeuchi and Nonaka's ideas. They developed the Scrum framework, drawing on their own experiences in software development and project management. Don't worry. The scrum frame diagram is all over the internet. I will have one in this book with a detailed explanation. Sutherland and Schwaber formalized Scrum in 1995, presenting it at the Object-Oriented

Programming, Systems, Languages, and Applications (OOPSLA) conference.

Scrum's early adopters were primarily in the software development industry, where the framework's iterative and adaptive nature proved particularly well-suited. As Scrum's popularity grew, it spread to other fields, including marketing, finance, and healthcare. In 2001, Schwaber and Sutherland co-founded the Scrum Alliance, a professional organization that promotes and supports Scrum practitioners. Scrum can be used in any industry as long as there is a product backlog.

The Scrum framework's core principles – teamwork, accountability, and iterative progress toward well-defined goals – resonated with organizations seeking to respond quickly to change. Scrum's emphasis on continuous improvement, customer satisfaction, and employee empowerment aligned with the values of the Agile movement, which emerged in the early 2000s. Today, Scrum is a cornerstone of Agile methodologies, widely adopted across industries and continents.

Throughout its evolution, Scrum has remained true to its rugby-inspired origins. The framework's nomenclature – Scrum, Sprint, Daily Scrum, and Scrum Master – reflects its sporting heritage. Scrum's iterative approach, where teams collaborate to achieve a common goal, mirrors rugby's dynamic, adaptive nature. As the business environment changes rapidly, Scrum's ability to facilitate teamwork, innovation, and swift response to change ensures its enduring relevance.

The Scrum framework's origin story is innovation and collaboration. From its roots in Japanese business scholarship to its adoption across industries, Scrum has remained a powerful tool for teams seeking to respond quickly to change and achieve their goals. As the business landscape evolves, Scrum's core principles and iterative approach will remain essential for organizations striving to stay ahead.

Waterfall vs Scrum

The Waterfall and Scrum methodologies are two distinct approaches to software development, each with its strengths and weaknesses. Both could utilize a Kanban board.

The Waterfall methodology is a traditional, linear approach to software development. It follows a sequential process, completing each phase before moving on to the next one. The phases typically include requirements gathering, design, implementation, testing, and deployment. Once a phase is completed, it's challenging to go back and make changes. This approach is often compared to a waterfall, where water flows down a steep slope, unable to turn back. "Some mfs are always trying to ice-skate uphill" - Blade

I prefer Scrum. Scrum is an Agile methodology that emphasizes flexibility and adaptability. Scrum involves iterative and incremental development, where the project is broken down into smaller chunks called Sprints. Each Sprint typically lasts 2-4 weeks and involves the entire development team. The team works on a specific set of tasks, and at the end of the Sprint, the work is reviewed, and feedback is gathered. Scrum allows for changes and adjustments throughout the development process, making it more responsive to customer needs. It's easier to change course if a new priority story comes into the product backlog.

AGILE VS. WATERFALL

Quick Comparison

Waterfall

Define › Design › Develop › Test › Deploy ›

FINAL OUTCOME

Agile

Test › Develop

Define › Design › Deploy ›

SPRINT'S OUTCOME

Test › Develop

Define › Design › Deploy ›

SPRINT'S CUMULATIVE OUTCOM

Test › Develop

Define › Design › Deploy ›

SPRINT'S CUMULATIVE OUTCOM

ASCEND MANAGEMENT GROUP

One of the primary differences between Waterfall and Scrum is the level of customer involvement. In Waterfall, customer requirements are gathered at the beginning of the project, and the development team works on implementing those requirements with little customer interaction. In Scrum, customers are actively involved throughout the development process, providing feedback and guidance at the end of each Sprint. Anyone can attend daily scrum, but not everyone can speak. If the stakeholder were to suggest a deviation from a sprint goal, the scrum master would have to protect the team from said deviation. The team is already committed.

Another significant difference is the approach to change management. Waterfall assumes that requirements are fixed and unchanging, whereas Scrum acknowledges that requirements can change rapidly. Scrum's iterative approach allows changes to be incorporated quickly without significant disruption to the project. This is called a Story Point Swap.

New priority work must start on the next sprint. The team should incorporate the latest stories into the current or upcoming sprint. For example, a new 3-point story would be "swapped" in and replace a less priority story that is also 3 points.

Waterfall's linear approach can lead to a higher risk of project failure due to the need for more flexibility. If requirements change or issues arise during development, adjusting the project scope without significant rework can be challenging. Developers can be left alone. Scrum's iterative approach mitigates this risk by allowing for continuous adaptation and adjustment. One reason is that every morning during daily scrum, developers are free to articulate any newly found defects, dependencies, or risks.

Scrum also promotes a more collaborative and self-organizing team culture. Team members work together to achieve Sprint goals, sharing responsibilities and expertise. It's a family raising a kid(software). In Waterfall, roles are often more defined, with less emphasis on teamwork and collaboration.

In terms of project planning, Waterfall relies on detailed upfront planning, whereas Scrum uses iterative planning. Scrum's planning is focused on the next Sprint rather than the entire project. This approach allows for greater flexibility and adaptability. Scrum works in small increments rather than focusing on a whole project.

Overall, Waterfall and Scrum represent fundamentally different approaches to software development. Waterfall's linear, predictable approach may suit projects with well-defined requirements and minimal risk. However, Scrum's iterative and adaptive approach is often more suitable for projects with rapidly changing requirements or high uncertainty.

By understanding the differences between Waterfall and Scrum, organizations can choose the methodology that best fits their project needs, ensuring successful software development and delivery. Nowadays, scrum makes more sense for most software development projects.

"We're gonna do Scrum, we're gonna be Agile." - Richard Hendricks - Silicon Valley (Season 1, Episode 3)

Scrum's flexibility, adaptability, and customer-centric approach have made it a popular choice for many organizations, particularly those in rapidly changing markets. Scrum's iterative and incremental approach will likely remain dominant as software development evolves.

Role of a Scrum Master

At the heart of the Scrum framework is the Scrum Master, a role responsible for facilitating team success. The Scrum Master is not a traditional project manager but a servant leader who empowers the team to self-organize and make decisions. Their primary focus is removing impediments, ensuring the Scrum process is followed, and fostering a collaborative environment. A Scrum Master is a coach and cheerleader for a scrum team. If you can create a Product Backlog, you can implement Scrum! Never miss an opportunity to coach a team member. Earn-your-keep . Now let's go!

The Scrum Master's responsibilities include:

Facilitating Scrum events, such as Sprint Planning, Daily Scrum, Sprint Review, and Sprint Retrospective. Ensuring the team understands and follows Scrum principles and practices. In some cases, conducting one-on-one training for team members that the Scrum Master recognizes don't understand Scrum Framework and Agile methodology. Removing impediments that obstruct the team's progress. Coaching team members in Scrum values, such as transparency, inspection, and adaptation. Protecting the team from external distractions and interruptions, encouraging continuous improvement and self-organization within the team.

Sometimes, a scrum master has to be creative in scheduling side meetings. The Scrum master has to ensure that the right resources (team members) attend the right meetings. For example, sometimes the dev team needs to be left alone to work; however, a representative is necessary for a particular meeting. In that case, just schedule the Lead Developer instead of the whole team for the meeting.

A successful Scrum Master possesses excellent communication, facilitation, and problem-solving skills. They must navigate conflicts, build trust, and empower team members to take ownership of their work. The Scrum Master is not responsible for assigning tasks or dictating how work should be done; instead, they focus on creating an environment where the team can thrive. Scrum Master is an oversight to ensure the team does not deviate from the framework and the stories they've committed to.

In addition to their core responsibilities, a Scrum Master may also:

Guide Scrum team on best practices and processes. Assist the Product Owner in refining the Product Backlog. Facilitate communication between stakeholders and the team. Identify and address team skill gaps or training needs. Monitor team velocity and progress, identifying areas for improvement while not acting like a boss or a manager. The Scrum Master is part of the team, not the team's superior.

By focusing on team empowerment and process facilitation, the Scrum Master enables the team to deliver high-quality products efficiently in increments. Influential Scrum Masters create a culture of collaboration, innovation, fun, and continuous improvement, allowing teams to respond quickly to changing requirements and achieve their goals.

"I'm the Scrum master, I'm the one who knows what's going on." - Dinesh Chugtai- Silicon Valley (Season 2, Episode 5)

The Scrum Master is vital in the Scrum framework, facilitating team success and ensuring the Scrum process is followed. 90% of a Scrum Master's conversation should be built around a Scrum event. To be honest, sometimes it feels like babysitting adults. By understanding the Scrum Master's responsibilities and skills, organizations can unlock the full potential of their teams and achieve greater agility and responsiveness in today's fast-paced business environment.

Agile principles and values

A gile is a mindset and approach to project management that emphasizes flexibility, collaboration, and rapid delivery. The Scrum masters should remind the team of at least one of these principles and values daily. At its core, Agile is built on four values and twelve principles, as outlined in the Agile Manifesto.

The four Agile values are:

Individuals and interactions over processes and tools.

Working software over comprehensive documentation.

Customer collaboration over contract negotiation.

Responding to change over following a plan.

These values prioritize people over process, working solutions, customer satisfaction, and adaptability. A Scrum Master should coach the team to embody these values by fostering a culture of collaboration, continuous improvement, and customer-centricity.

The twelve Agile principles guide how to implement these values. They include:

Satisfy the customer through early and continuous delivery of valuable software

Welcome changing requirements, even late in development

Deliver working software frequently, from a couple of weeks to a couple of months

Business people and developers must work together daily

Build projects around motivated individuals, giving them the environment and support they need

The most efficient and effective method of conveying information is face-to-face conversation

Working software is the primary measure of progress

Agile processes promote sustainable development, the ability to maintain a constant pace

Continuous attention to technical excellence and good design enhances agility

Simplicity—the art of maximizing the amount of work not done—is essential

The best architectures, requirements, and designs emerge from self-organizing teams

Regularly, the team reflects on how to become more agile

A Scrum Master should coach the Scrum team to embrace these principles by:

Encouraging active customer involvement and feedback

Embracing change and adapting to new requirements

Focusing on delivering working software in short iterations

Fostering collaboration and communication among team members and stakeholders

Empowering team members to take ownership and make decisions

Promoting face-to-face communication and minimizing documentation

Prioritizing technical excellence and simplicity

Encouraging continuous improvement and reflection

By coaching the Scrum team to embrace Agile values and principles, a Scrum Master can help the team become more responsive, adaptable, and customer-focused, leading to tremendous success and satisfaction. When I send an Email to my Scrum Team, an Agile Principle or Value is usually the first line of my email.

Scrum Facilitator

E ffective facilitators are crucial to the success of Scrum events, ensuring productive and efficient meetings that drive collaboration and decision-making. A skilled Scrum facilitator embodies the principles of assertiveness, servant leadership, and clear communication. This person leads by example and always speaks in scrum vernacular. The Scrum master is also a master note-taker.

Assertiveness is crucial in facilitating Scrum events. The facilitator must confidently guide the discussion, keep the meeting on track, and ensure all voices are heard. This requires setting clear expectations, establishing a positive tone, and maintaining control without being authoritarian. An assertive facilitator intervenes when necessary, redirects conversations, and prevents domination by individual team members. Sometimes, you just have to tell people to take the conversation "offline" if time runs out for the meeting or the subject is off-topic. There are ways to redirect conversation without being rude.

Servant leadership is equally essential. The facilitator's primary goal is to serve the team, enabling them to achieve their objectives. This involves creating a safe, trustworthy, inclusive environment, fostering open communication, and empowering team members to take ownership. A servant-leader facilitator prioritizes the team's needs, provides guidance, and removes impediments.

Effective facilitation also relies on clear articulation of rules of engagement. Before the meeting, the facilitator communicates the objectives, agenda, and expected outcomes. They reiterate these guidelines during the event, ensuring all participants understand the norms and expectations. This includes establishing ground rules, such as active listening, respectful dialogue, and no interruptions.

To articulate rules of engagement, the facilitator might say:

"Welcome, everyone. Before we begin, let's establish some ground rules to ensure productive discussion. We'll respect each other's opinions, listen actively, and avoid interruptions. We'll also keep our discussions focused on the agenda items. If you have a question or concern, please don't hesitate to raise it."

Presentation tools are vital for effective facilitation. Scrum facilitators use visual aids to engage participants, illustrate concepts, and track progress. These tools may include:

Whiteboards or sticky notes for brainstorming and idea mapping

Digital collaboration platforms like Mural, Google Jamboard, or Microsoft Whiteboard

Visual facilitation techniques, such as graphic recording or sketching, noting

Agile project management tools like Jira, Trello, or Asana

During Scrum events, the facilitator employs these tools to:

Illustrate complex concepts and relationships

Track progress and action items

Facilitate group discussions and decision-making

Create a shared understanding of goals and objectives

For example, during Sprint Planning, the facilitator might use a whiteboard or Jira to visualize the Product Backlog, dependencies, and team capacity. This visual representation enables the team to understand the workflow better, identify potential roadblocks, and prioritize tasks effectively.

In addition to presentation tools, effective facilitators leverage active listening skills, asking open-ended questions to encourage participation and clarify understanding. They also recognize and address conflicts respectfully, navigating difficult conversations with empathy and professionalism.

To ensure successful Scrum events, facilitators must:

Prepare thoroughly, reviewing objectives, agendas, and relevant materials

Create a conducive environment, minimizing distractions and promoting focus

Encourage participation, recognizing and valuing diverse perspectives

Maintain flexibility, adapting to changing circumstances and emerging issues

Scrum facilitators create an environment conducive to collaboration, innovation, and success by embodying assertiveness, servant leadership, and clear communication. By leveraging practical presentation tools and articulating rules of engagement, they ensure productive and efficient meetings that drive Scrum teams forward.

Effective facilitation is the definition of Scrum success. By mastering assertiveness, servant leadership, and clear communication, facilitators empower Scrum teams to achieve their objectives. By utilizing presentation tools and articulating rules of engagement, facilitators create an environment that fosters collaboration, enjoyment, innovation, and productivity.

Meet your Scrum Team

Hi, I'm the Product Owner. I'm responsible for defining and prioritizing the product backlog, ensuring it is up-to-date and refined. My relationship with the team is collaborative, as I work closely with them to understand their capabilities and constraints. I provide clear guidance on the product vision and requirements, and the team relies on me for clarification and feedback. My relationship with the Scrum Master is also vital, as they help facilitate communication and ensure the team is working efficiently. Scrum master is my right-hand "person."

Hi, I'm the Scrum Master. I facilitate Scrum processes and ensure the team follows the framework. My role is to enable the team to work efficiently, removing impediments and fostering a collaborative environment. I work closely with the Product Owner to understand their needs and ensure the team is aligned with the product vision. I also coach the team on Scrum principles and practices, helping them continuously improve. As Scrum Master, I will oversee the project and make sure the team has the tools and the candance to be successful.

Hi, I'm a Development Team Member. I'm responsible for developing and delivering working software in each sprint. I collaborate with the team to design, develop, and test the product. I work closely with the Product Owner to understand requirements and ensure we meet customer needs. I also rely on the Scrum Master to facilitate our processes and remove obstacles. As a team, we share knowledge, skills, and expertise to deliver high-quality software.

Hi, I'm another Development Team Member with specialized skills. I may be a software tester (QA) or a software architect. I'm responsible for bringing my expertise to the team, whether in design, testing, or architecture. I collaborate with the team to ensure our deliverables meet the highest standards. I work closely with the Product Owner to understand requirements and ensure we meet customer needs. I also rely on the Scrum Master to facilitate our processes and remove obstacles.

Hi, I'm a Stakeholder. I'm responsible for providing input and feedback on the product. I collaborate with the Product Owner to ensure the product meets customer needs. I work closely with the Scrum Master to understand the team's progress and provide guidance. I also rely on the Development Team to deliver high-quality software that meets my expectations. As a stakeholder, I trust the team to make decisions and deliver value, and I'm available to provide guidance and support when needed. I try not to interrupt the team's progress with new requirements.

A Scrum team typically consists of 3-9 members, each with distinct roles and responsibilities. The Product Owner is at the team's heart and is responsible for defining and prioritizing the product backlog. This individual ensures that the team understands the product vision and requirements and that the backlog is up-to-date, refined, and ready.

The Scrum Master is the glue that holds the team together and ensures the team follows the framework. This person removes impediments (blockers), fosters a collaborative environment, and coaches the team on Scrum principles and practices. The Scrum Master works closely with the Product Owner to understand their needs and ensures the team is aligned with the product vision. Sometimes, the Scrum Master brings the team coffee and donuts.

The Development Team comprises 3-7 members with unique skills and expertise. These individuals collaborate to design, develop, and test the product, working together to deliver high-quality software in each sprint. The Development Team may include Software Engineers, Developers, QA Engineers, UX Designers, and DevOps Engineers. While titles may vary, the team shares a common goal: to deliver working software that meets customer needs based on requirements.

A Scrum team may sometimes include additional roles, such as a Technical Lead, Design Lead, or QA Lead. These individuals guide and oversee their respective areas, ensuring the team delivers high-quality software that meets the required standards. However, it's essential to remember that Scrum teams are self-organizing and honest, and roles may overlap or evolve as needed.

The Scrum framework emphasizes collaboration, flexibility, and shared responsibility. Team members work together, share knowledge and expertise, and make collective decisions to achieve their goals. The Scrum team is not a collection of individuals working in silos; instead, it's a cohesive unit that relies on open communication, trust, and mutual respect. I am unafraid to keep the development conversation over other collaboration tools. By working together, the Scrum team delivers high-quality software that meets customer needs and drives business success.

Scrum Team Agreement

In Scrum, a Team Agreement is a shared understanding among team members outlining expectations, behaviors, and working practices. It fosters collaboration, accountability, and transparency, ensuring everyone is aligned and working towards common goals. A well-crafted Team Agreement promotes a positive and productive team culture.

Creating a Team Agreement typically occurs during Program Increment (PI) Planning or before Sprint Planning. The Scrum Master facilitates a workshop where team members and stakeholders gather to discuss and define the agreement. This collaborative process encourages active listening, inclusivity, and consensus-building. The Scrum Master ensures that all voices are heard and that the deal reflects the team's unique needs and dynamics.

A comprehensive Team Agreement includes guidelines for communication, collaboration, meeting norms, decision-making processes, conflict resolution, feedback, quality standards, work hours, and vacation policies. It also outlines expectations for continuous improvement and learning. By explicitly stating these guidelines, team members understand their responsibilities and can be held accountable for adhering to the agreement.

The Scrum Master creates the Team Agreement, facilitating open discussions and ensuring the agreement is realistic, achievable, and aligned with the team's goals. They document and visualize the deal, making it easily accessible to all team members. Regular reviews and updates ensure the agreement remains relevant and practical.

Throughout the Scrum framework, the Team Agreement serves as a reference point. During Sprint Planning, it ensures alignment with team goals and expectations. Daily Scrum helps address impediments or deviations from the agreement. Sprint Review evaluates progress and adherence to quality standards, while Sprint Retrospective reflects on team dynamics, processes, and agreement adherence. The Retrospective provides an opportunity to identify areas for improvement and update the agreement as needed.

By embracing a Team Agreement, Scrum teams cultivate accountability, transparency, collaboration, continuous improvement, and adaptability. This foundational document empowers team members to work together effectively, fostering a culture of trust, respect, and shared responsibility.

Example of a Scrum Team Agreement:

Team Name: Pied Piper Development Team

Purpose: Collaborate to deliver high-quality software solutions, prioritizing transparency, accountability, and continuous improvement.

Communication:

- Respond to messages within 2 hours during work hours

- Use Slack for team communication

- Escalate critical issues to Scrum Master

Meetings:

- Daily Scrum: 10:00 AM, 15-minute time-box

- Sprint Planning: 2 hours, every 2 weeks

- Sprint Review: 1 hour, every 2 weeks

- Sprint Retrospective: 1.5 hours, every 2 weeks

Collaboration:

- Pair programming encouraged for complex tasks

- Code reviews within 24 hours

- Active participation in meetings

Decision-Making:

- Consensus-driven

- Majority vote if consensus unreachable

Quality Standards:

- Follow coding standards and best practices

- Unit testing for all new code

- Peer review for critical components

Work Hours and Availability:

- 10:00 AM - 6:00 PM, Monday - Friday

- Notify the team of vacations or absences 2 weeks in advance

Continuous Improvement:

- Regularly seek feedback

- Attend workshops and training sessions

- Share knowledge and expertise

Conflict Resolution:

- Address issues promptly

- Escalate to Scrum Master if unresolved

Review and Update:

- Review agreement every 6 sprints

- Update as needed

This example outlines basic guidelines for communication, meetings, collaboration, decision-making, quality standards, work hours, continuous improvement, conflict resolution, and review processes. The team should agree to this code of conduct to have a shared understanding of what is expected of each member.

Program Increment (PI Planning) and the Scrum Master

A Program Increment (PI) is a critical component of the Scaled Agile Framework (SAFe), representing a long-term plan for a team or multiple teams working together to achieve a set of goals and objectives. Typically spanning 8-12 weeks, a PI provides a framework for teams to collaborate, innovate, and deliver high-quality software that meets customer needs.

During a Program Increment, a Scrum Master's conduct ensures the teams' success. Their primary responsibility is facilitating PI planning, a critical event where teams come together to plan and align on the work for the upcoming increment. The Scrum Master works closely with the teams, Product Owners, and stakeholders to ensure everyone is aligned and working towards the same objectives. Sometimes, people are not aligned. The Scrum Master must actively listen to people and connect them to the proper channel to resolve any issues.

As the PI unfolds, the Scrum Master focuses on ensuring team alignment and progress. They work with teams to ensure they are on track to meet their commitments, identifying and removing impediments blocking progress. This involves coaching teams on Agile principles and practices, facilitating Scrum events, and collaborating with the Release Train Engineer (RTE) to ensure team alignment.

Facilitating Scrum events is critical to the Scrum Master's role during a PI. They ensure that teams follow the Scrum framework, promoting events such as Sprint Planning, Daily Scrum, Sprint Review, and Sprint Retrospective. This helps teams stay focused, aligned, and committed to delivering high-quality software.

Monitoring progress is another critical responsibility of the Scrum Master during a PI. They track teams' progress, identifying areas where teams may need support or guidance. This involves working closely with teams, Product Owners, and stakeholders to ensure everyone is informed and aligned.

Throughout the PI, the Scrum Master collaborates with the RTE to ensure team alignment. They work together to identify and address dependencies, ensure teams work towards the same objectives, and facilitate communication across teams.

In PI Planning, the Scrum master will ensure the team understands the objective for the next quarter. The Scrum Master partners with the Product Owner to draft the team's work capacity for at least the first and the second sprint. Also, possible risks could occur while preparing stories for DoR (Definition of Ready) before kicking off the first sprint.

Outputs of PI Planning

I'm stressing PI Planning because your team will work optimally if you get a solid start. The output of PI planning is a comprehensive plan that outlines the objectives, goals, and deliverables for the upcoming Program Increment. One of the key outputs is the team capacity plan, which outlines the available capacity for each team participating in the PI. This plan considers the team's velocity, availability, and workload to ensure they are appropriately committed and utilized.

The team capacity plan is closely tied to the load plan, which outlines the estimated effort required to complete the planned work. The load plan ensures the team's capacity is aligned with the workload, preventing overloading and potential burnout. By understanding the team's capacity and load, leaders can make informed decisions about resource allocation and prioritize work accordingly. If the workload is 50 story points but the team Capacity is 35, the Product Owner must move 15 story points of less priority stories to the next sprint.

Another critical output of PI planning is the identification of exterior team dependencies. These dependencies represent the essential interfaces between teams that require coordination and collaboration to deliver the PI objectives. By identifying these dependencies, teams can proactively manage relationships with external teams, ensure alignment, and mitigate potential risks. Some items may only be able to be worked on if another team completes a part of an API and hands it off. These interactions need to be coordinated.

The PI plan also includes a comprehensive roadmap of the increment's key milestones, deliverables, and objectives. This roadmap clearly represents the work, enabling teams to stay focused and aligned throughout the PI.

In addition to the team capacity, load, and dependency plans, the PI planning output includes a set of agreed-upon PI objectives. These objectives are specific, measurable, achievable, relevant, and time-bound (SMART) goals that align with the organization's strategic vision. By focusing on these objectives, teams can ensure that their work is aligned with the organization's priorities and that they deliver value to customers.

The final output of PI planning is a shared understanding and commitment among teams to deliver the planned work. This shared understanding is critical to ensuring that teams work collaboratively, manage dependencies effectively, and adapt to changes throughout the PI.

Overall, the output of PI planning provides a comprehensive framework for teams to collaborate, innovate, and deliver high-quality software that meets customer needs. By understanding team capacity, load, exterior team dependencies, and PI objectives, leaders can make informed decisions, prioritize work, and ensure the successful delivery of the Program Increment.

The PI planning output also includes key metrics and indicators that will be used to measure progress and success throughout the increment. These metrics may include cycle time, lead time, and defect density, providing visibility into the team's performance and enabling data-driven decision-making.

By documenting and communicating the PI planning output, leaders can ensure that all stakeholders are informed and aligned, setting the stage for a successful Program Increment.

Definition of Done (DoD)

Now let's talk about The Definition of Done (DoD). It's a concept in Scrum that ensures consistency in quality and standards across all Product Backlog items. It represents a shared understanding among team members of what it means for an item to be considered complete. As a Scrum Master, articulating and coaching this concept to the team is essential for achieving high-quality deliverables. The Scrum Master begins by facilitating a team discussion to define their DoD, ensuring everyone understands the criteria to be met for an item to be considered.

"The Definition of Done is not just a checklist," the Scrum Master explains. "It's a mindset shift towards delivering quality software that meets our standards." The team brainstorms and agrees on criteria such as code reviewed and tested, meeting acceptance criteria, documented, and deployed to production. The Scrum Master emphasizes that DoD is not a one-time activity but an ongoing process that evolves as the team grows and learns. However, DoD could be as simple as a checklist. Example: " Design - Build - Test. DONE!

To reinforce this concept, the Scrum Master encourages the team to ask themselves during Sprint Review: "Is this item truly done? Does it meet our Definition of Done?" This simple yet powerful question fosters a culture of accountability and quality. The Scrum Master also ensures that the DoD is visible and accessible to all team members, often displayed prominently on the team's collaboration board, wiki, or even a signed Team Agreement.

By coaching the team on the Definition of Done, the Scrum Master empowers them to take honest ownership of their work and strive for excellence. As the team adopts this mindset, they begin to deliver high-quality software that meets customer expectations, and the organization benefits from increased reliability, maintainability, and customer satisfaction. The team solidifies its commitment to quality and excellence through continuous refinement and adherence to its Definition of Done.

Definition of Ready (DoR)

As your Scrum Master, I want to emphasize the importance of the Definition of Ready (DoR) in our Scrum framework. The DoR represents a shared understanding among team members of when a Product Backlog item is ready for development. It's a critical concept that ensures clarity and alignment on requirements, allowing us to develop high-quality software that meets customer needs based on requirements.

Think of the DoR as a checklist that ensures we've done our due diligence before starting work on a Product Backlog item. It's not just about having a clear description of the item; it's about having a deep understanding and conversation during PI Planning, Sprint Planning, and Backlog Refinement of what needs to be done, why it needs to be done, and how it aligns with our product vision.

So, what does it mean for an item to be "ready"? Typically, the item has well-defined acceptance criteria, estimated effort in story points, is prioritized, and aligns with our product vision. Let's break this down further, shall we?

Well-defined acceptance criteria mean that we clearly understand what success looks like for this item. The product owner should be confident that the team has the skill set to understand and complete the item. What conditions are required for us to consider this item complete? We ensure everyone on the team is on the same page, and we're not interpreting requirements differently.

Estimated effort in story points allows us to understand the complexity and scope of the work involved. This helps us plan our Sprints more effectively and ensures we pay attention to ourselves. Most ambitious teams try to take on more work than their historic velocity. Scrum Master would step and not allow this to happen.

Prioritization is critical to ensure we're first working on the most valuable items. By prioritizing our Product Backlog, we're making conscious decisions about where to focus our efforts and aligning with the PO's vision. I would always recommend that the team resolve difficult items first. A Scrum master should know and hold the Product Owner accountable for stories or work items at the agreed DoR.

Finally, aligning with our product vision ensures we achieve a common goal. We're not just developing software for the sake of developing software; we're developing software that meets customer requirements and aligns with our organization's objectives.

By having a shared understanding of the DoR, we can ensure that we're developing high-quality software that meets customer requirements. As your Scrum Master, I encourage you to ask yourselves during Sprint Planning: "Is this item ready for development? Does it meet our Definition of Ready?" Let's work together to ensure we deliver software that makes a difference and works.

As a product owner, acceptance criteria are crucial to ensuring that the product backlog items meet the required standards and customer needs. Acceptance criteria represent conditions that must be met for a Product Backlog item to be considered complete. These criteria serve as a checklist to evaluate whether the item meets the requirements and delivers the expected value.

Acceptance Criteria

Acceptance criteria are typically defined during the Product Backlog refinement process, where the Product Owner works closely with stakeholders and the Development Team to ensure that everyone has a shared understanding of what needs to be done. These criteria are usually specific, measurable, achievable, relevant, and time-bound (SMART), making it clear what success looks like for each item.

For example, let's say we have a Product Backlog item to develop a new login feature. The acceptance criteria for this item might include conditions such as:

- The login feature must authenticate users within 2 seconds.

- The feature must support multiple authentication methods (e.g., username/password, social media, biometrics).

- The feature must be accessible on both desktop and mobile devices.

- The feature must comply with industry-standard security protocols.

By defining these acceptance criteria, the Product Owner ensures that the Development Team understands what is required to complete the item. During Sprint Review, the team can evaluate whether the item meets these criteria and, if not, discuss what needs to be done to complete it.

Acceptance criteria also help prevent scope creep and ensure the team is not overcommitting themselves. By having clear criteria, the team can focus on delivering the required functionality without getting sidetracked by non-essential features.

Ok, Listen. The AC is a way to let the PO know that the item is done. The PO needs to use the Acceptance or AC to test the item to see if it works and meets requirements. For example, there should be an AC list for every story. The list should be easy to follow to show the PO that the item is working as expected. The Product Owner will test the item using the AC. If the item does not follow the AC, then the PO will send it back to the developer to be fixed, which is not a good look for the developer.

Moreover, acceptance criteria facilitate communication and collaboration between the Product Owner, Development Team, and stakeholders. They provide a common language and understanding of what needs to be done, reducing misunderstandings and misinterpretations.

Acceptance criteria ensure product backlog items meet the required standards and customer needs. By defining specific conditions that must be met, Product Owners can evaluate whether items meet requirements, prevent scope creep, and facilitate effective communication and collaboration. As a Product Owner, it is crucial to invest time and effort in defining clear and concise acceptance criteria to guarantee the delivery of high-quality software that meets customer expectations.

Story Pointing (Estimating)

Scrum Masters coaching a Scrum team on story pointing ensures effective sprint planning and estimation. Story pointing estimates the effort required to complete a Product Backlog item, and teams must understand the importance of honesty and transparency during this process.

Story pointing uses relative estimation, such as the Fibonacci sequence (0, 1, 2, 3, 5, 8, 13, etc.), to estimate the effort required to complete an item. This approach helps teams avoid absolute estimates, which can be misleading and unreliable. Instead, relative estimation encourages teams to think about complexity and scope. A Zero point story could be a backlog item the team should monitor during a sprint. The story could be a task that needs to be followed up on during the sprint. Usually, 1 point represents an 8-hour work day in a real-world scrum scenario. However, Scrum's text would say, "Estimating is not estimating hours or days."

During sprint planning, the team reviews each Product Backlog item and assigns a story point value based on the estimated effort required. The Scrum Master's role is to facilitate this process, ensuring that the team understands the importance of honesty and transparency.

"It's not about getting it exactly right," the Scrum Master explains. "It's about being consistent, honest, and relative in your estimation. We're not estimating hours or days; we're estimating complexity." The team nods, understanding that story-pointing is a collaborative effort. The team needs to agree with the estimates of each story. If there is a disagreement, allow the team member to express concerns about the overestimate or under-estimate. The team or even the rogue team member could concede after an explanation. If there is no strong argument, then "the team has spoken," and the story will be pointed based on what most of the team has agreed on.

As the team begins estimating, the Scrum Master encourages them to ask questions and clarify assumptions. "What do you mean by 'complex'?" a team member asks. "Is it the number of lines of code, the number of integrations, or something else?" The team discusses and agrees on what complexity means for each item. Complexity could be based on the skill set of the team.

The Scrum Master reminds the team that story-pointing is not a competition. Be honest. "We're not trying to one-up each other with higher estimates," they say. "We're working together to understand the effort required." This helps to create a safe and open environment where team members feel comfortable sharing their thoughts. It's okay to be ambitious; however, only sign up for what you can handle.

When a team member suggests a high estimate, the Scrum Master asks, "What makes you think this item is an 8?" The team member explains their reasoning, and the team discusses and adjusts the estimate accordingly. The scrum master should recommend breaking up an 8-point story into 2-3-3. It would be easier for the team to take on. An 8-point story would occupy a single team member for an entire sprint. Why not let the whole team tackle parts of the item?

Through this process, the team develops a shared understanding of the effort required to complete each item. The Scrum Master emphasizes that story-pointing is not a one-time activity but an ongoing process that evolves as the team grows and learns. It's one of the ways for a team to be self-organizing and predictable.

As the team becomes more comfortable with story-pointing, they recognize patterns and trends. They realize that certain types of tasks consistently require more effort than others. This insight enables them to refine their estimation process and improve their sprint planning. This is the purpose of the scrum framework and agile methodology.

The Scrum Master reinforces the importance of being honest and transparent during story pointing. "If you're unsure or don't understand an item, don't be afraid to say so," they advise. "We can always break it down or seek clarification." This encourages team members to speak up and ensures that estimates are realistic and achievable.

By coaching the team on story-pointing, the Scrum Master helps them develop a robust estimation process that fosters collaboration, predictability, transparency, and accountability. As the team becomes more proficient in story-pointing, they can plan more effectively, manage their workload, and deliver high-quality software that meets customer expectations.

Understanding the Story pointing is a significant aspect of Scrum, and the Scrum Master plays a considerable role in coaching the team to understand its importance. By emphasizing honesty, transparency, and relative estimation, the Scrum Master helps the team develop a robust estimation process that drives effective sprint planning and delivery.

User Stories

Ser Stories are a fundamental component of Agile product development, clearly and concisely describing Product Backlog items from the user's perspective. This approach ensures that the Development Team understands the requirements and needs of the end-user, enabling them to deliver software that meets customer expectations.

A well-crafted User Story typically follows a simple yet effective format: "As a [user], I want [feature] so that [benefit]." This structure forces the team to consider the user's role, the desired feature, and the underlying benefit that the feature provides. Don't take this lightly. It makes a well-rounded user story so that everyone can understand the application.

For example, a User Story for an e-commerce application might read: "As a customer, I want to be able to track my order status online so that I can stay informed about delivery times." This story clearly articulates the user's need, the desired feature, and the benefit of having that feature. The team and the PO will understand this as well.

By focusing on the user's perspective, User Stories help the Development Team to prioritize requirements based on customer value. This approach ensures that the team delivers software that meets the target audience's needs.

User Stories also facilitate effective communication among stakeholders. Product Owners, Developers, and Designers can discuss and refine the requirements, ensuring that everyone shares a common understanding of what needs to be delivered.

When writing User Stories, it's essential to keep them concise, specific, and measurable. Avoid vague or overly broad statements that may confuse the Development Team. Instead, break down complex requirements into smaller, manageable stories. I said this before. Break down stories that are estimated high into smaller stories.

User Stories descriptions often use acceptance criteria to provide additional context and clarity. These criteria outline the conditions that must be met for the story to be considered complete. A User Stories description is different. One is for understanding the story, and the other is for testing.

For instance, the acceptance criteria for the order tracking story might include:

- The user can log in to their account and view order status.

- The order status is updated in real time.

- The user receives email notifications when the order status changes.

Those are walkthrough steps to make sure it's working as intended. So, a product owner can "accept" the developer's work, which is part of the definition of done.

By combining User Stories with Acceptance Criteria, teams can ensure they deliver high-quality software that meets customer needs.

User Stories provide a framework for describing Product Backlog items from the user's perspective. By following the simple yet effective format of "As a [user], I want [feature] so that [benefit]," teams can ensure that they're delivering software that meets customer expectations and provides real value. Don't overthink it.

User Stories enables teams to prioritize requirements, communicate effectively, and deliver software that delights customers. As a critical component of Agile product development, User Stories is vital in driving successful software development projects.

INVEST Criteria

I want you to be a Mr. or Ms. Know-it-all at work. I want you to shine at every endeavor and have input whenever an opportunity arises. The INVEST criteria are guidelines for writing practical Product Backlog items, ensuring that they meet the necessary standards for successful Agile software development. You want to "earn your keep" as a Scrum Master. When you speak, make sure you are coaching the team. Coach the team on the INVEST Criteria. Each letter in the INVEST acronym represents a critical characteristic that Product Backlog items should possess.

I - Independent

Independent Product Backlog items are free from dependencies, allowing the Development Team to work on them without being hindered by other items. Each item can be developed, tested, and deployed independently without affecting other items in the backlog.

For example, consider a Product Backlog item to implement a payment gateway. If this item is dependent on another item, such as integrating a third-party API, it's not independent. The team could break it down into smaller items to make it independent, such as developing the payment gateway UI and integrating the API as separate items.

N - Negotiable

Negotiable Product Backlog items allow flexibility and discussion between the Product Owner and the Development

Team. This characteristic ensures that items are not set in stone, enabling the team to refine and adjust requirements.

A negotiable item might be: "As a customer, I want to be able to track my order status online." The Development Team can discuss and refine this requirement with the Product Owner, ensuring the solution meets customer needs.

V - Valuable

Valuable Product Backlog items provide tangible benefits to customers, stakeholders, or the business. This characteristic ensures that each item contributes to the overall product vision and goals.

For instance, a valuable item might be: "Implementing two-factor authentication to enhance customer security." This item provides clear value to customers by protecting their accounts.

E - Estimable

The Development Team can accurately estimate Estimable Product Backlog items. This characteristic ensures that the team can plan and prioritize work effectively.

An estimable item might be: "Develop a new UI component for the login page." The Development Team can estimate the effort required to complete this task based on their expertise and experience.

S - Small

Small Product Backlog items are granular and manageable, allowing the Development Team to complete them within a single Sprint. This characteristic ensures that progress is measurable and incremental.

A small item might be: "Update the footer text on the website." This item is concise and can be completed quickly.

T - Testable

Testable Product Backlog items have clear acceptance criteria, enabling the Development Team to verify that the item meets requirements. This characteristic ensures that the team delivers high-quality software. Get this conversation going in PI planning, Sprint Planning, and Product Backlog.

A testable item might be: "Implement password reset functionality." The acceptance criteria could include:

- The user receives an email with a password reset link.

- The password reset link expires after 30 minutes.

- The user can successfully reset their password.

By applying the INVEST criteria, Product Owners and Development Teams can ensure that Product Backlog items are well-defined, effective, and aligned with Agile principles. This leads to better planning, estimation, and delivery of software that meets customer needs.

The INVEST criteria provide a framework for crafting high-quality Product Backlog items. By ensuring that items are independent, Negotiated, valuable, Escalationable, small, and testable, teams can deliver software that provides real value to customers and stakeholders. Practical application of INVEST criteria enables teams to work efficiently, prioritize requirements, and drive successful software development projects.

SMART

S MART Scrum integrates the SMART (Specific, Measurable, Achievable, Relevant, Time-bound) criteria with Scrum principles to ensure well-defined and actionable goals. I have this concept in mind during Sprint Retrospective, Sprint Planning, and Backlog Refinement. I'm always ready to coach the team on this.

SMART Criteria in Scrum:

1. Specific: Clearly define Sprint Goals, Product Backlog items, and tasks to avoid ambiguity.

Example: Instead of "Improve user experience," use "Increase login success rate by 20%."

2. Measurable: Quantify goals and progress to track success.

Example: "Reduce average bug resolution time to 2 hours" instead of "Improve bug resolution."

3. Achievable: Ensure goals are realistic and attainable based on team velocity and capacity.

Example: Set realistic Sprint Goals considering the team's historical velocity.

4. Relevant: Align goals with the product vision, business objectives, and customer needs.

Example: Prioritize features based on customer feedback and market demands.

5. Time-bound: Establish deadlines for Sprints, tasks, and milestones.

Example: Set a specific Sprint duration (e.g., 2 weeks) with defined start and end dates.

Benefits of SMART Scrum:

1. Improved focus and clarity

2. Enhanced team collaboration and communication

3. Increased productivity and efficiency

4. Better prioritization and decision-making

5. More accurate forecasting and planning

Applying SMART Scrum:

1. Product Owner: Ensures Product Backlog items meet SMART criteria.

2. Scrum Master: Facilitates SMART goal-setting and follows Scrum principles.

3. Development Team: Break down SMART goals into actionable tasks.

Tools for SMART Scrum:

1. Jira, Trello, or Asana for task management

2. Confluence or Notion for documentation

3. Google Analytics or metrics tools for measurement

4. Sprint planning and review templates

By incorporating SMART criteria into Scrum, teams can create clear, actionable, and achievable goals, improving productivity, quality, and customer satisfaction.

References:

- "Scrum: The Art of Doing Twice the Work in Half the Time" by Jeff Sutherland

- "Agile Project Management with Scrum" by Ken Schwaber

- "SMART Goals" by George T. Doran

Community of Practice (CoP)

A Community of Practice (CoP) meeting for Scrum Masters is a valuable opportunity for professionals to share knowledge, experiences, and best practices in Scrum framework implementation. Don't ever expose yourself to not knowing certain aspects of scrum. However, a Scrum Masters safe space is a CoP. As a Scrum Master, conducting such a meeting involves creating a collaborative environment where peers can discuss challenges, exchange ideas, and learn from each other's successes and failures.

The meeting begins with an icebreaker, where participants share their challenges and goals, setting the stage for meaningful discussions. The Scrum Master facilitator then introduces the agenda, which may include scaling Scrum, handling difficult team members, or implementing Scrum in complex environments. The facilitator uses techniques like Open Space or World Café to encourage active participation, allowing participants to self-organize and drive the conversations. Here's another tip: Find trustworthy "allies" within the organization and form your own CoP. You will be able to ask your obscure questions there.

As the meeting progresses, Scrum Masters share their experiences, asking questions and offering advice. For instance, one Scrum Master may discuss their approach to prioritizing the Product Backlog, while another shares their technique for facilitating effective Sprint Planning. The group engages in lively debates, exploring different perspectives and approaches. The facilitator ensures the discussions remain focused and productive, encouraging participants to share their thoughts and insights.

A vital aspect of the CoP meeting is the opportunity for Scrum Masters to collaborate on solving real-world problems. Participants work together to address common challenges, sharing their expertise and experience. This will make you a better Scrum Master, learning directly from your peers in real time. This collective problem-solving approach fosters community and camaraderie, as Scrum Masters recognize that they face similar obstacles and can learn from each other's experiences.

Throughout the meeting, the facilitator captures vital takeaways, action items, and ideas for future discussions. This ensures that the community continues to learn and grow, with each meeting building upon the previous one. As the meeting concludes, participants leave with renewed energy, new ideas, and a deeper understanding of Scrum principles and practices. The CoP meeting is a valuable platform for Scrum Masters to grow professionally, driving improvements in their teams and organizations. I will add again the importance of creating your own personal CoP amongst trustworthy allies within the organization or even having a one-on-one meeting with an Agile Coach if you need scrum questions answered. I would not ask RTE anything about scrum. It's not a good look.

Time Box

As a Scrum Master, enforcing time boxes for Scrum events ensures productivity, focus, and efficiency. You will have to interrupt conversations in Scrum Events to advise attendees that "This meeting is time-boxed; you may have to take your queries offline." Here are typical time boxes for Scrum events:

Sprint Planning (Time Box: 1-2 hours)

- Duration: 1 hour for 1-week Sprints, 2 hours for 2-4 week Sprints

- Objective: Set Sprint Goal, select Product Backlog items and plan tasks

Daily Scrum, Stand-up (Time Box: 15 minutes)

- Duration: 15 minutes, same time every day

- Objective: Share progress, plans, and impediments

Sprint Review (Time Box: 1-2 hours)

- Duration: 1 hour for 1-week Sprints, 2 hours for 2-4 week Sprints

- Objective: Showcase accomplishments, receive feedback, and discuss next steps

Sprint Retrospective (Time Box: 1-2 hours)

- Duration: 1 hour for 1-week Sprints, 2 hours for 2-4 week Sprints

- Objective: Reflect on processes, identify improvements, and implement changes

Backlog Refinement (Time Box: 1-2 hours)

- Duration: 1-2 hours; frequency varies (e.g., weekly or bi-weekly)

- Objective: Review, refine, and prioritize Product Backlog items

Scrum of Scrums (Time Box: 15-30 minutes)

- Duration: 15-30 minutes; frequency varies (e.g., daily or weekly)

- Objective: Coordinate multiple Scrum teams, discuss dependencies, and align efforts

Enforcing time boxes ensures:

- Focus on key objectives

- Efficient use of team members' time

- Productive discussions and decision-making

- Respect for attendees' time and schedules

As the Scrum Master, it's essential to:

- Communicate time boxes clearly to attendees

- Start and end meetings on time

- Manage discussions to stay within time boxes

- Adapt time boxes as needed, based on team feedback and changing requirements

By enforcing time boxes, the Scrum Master maintains a structured and productive environment, enabling the team to deliver high-quality software efficiently.

Scrum Artifacts

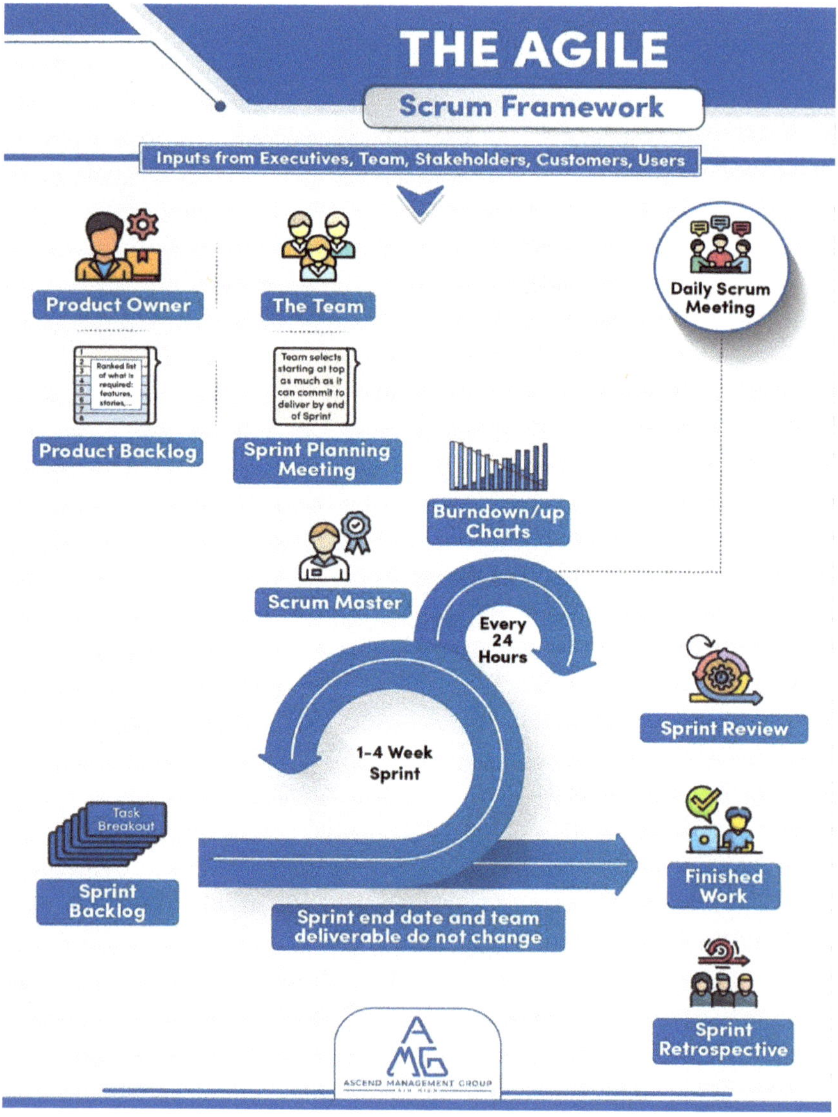

THE AGILE

Scrum Framework

Inputs from Executives, Team, Stakeholders, Customers, Users

Product Owner

The Team

Daily Scrum Meeting

Ranked list of what is required: features, stories,...

Product Backlog

Team selects starting at top as much as it can commit to deliver by end of Sprint

Sprint Planning Meeting

Burndown/up Charts

Scrum Master

Every 24 Hours

1-4 Week Sprint

Sprint Review

Task Breakout

Sprint Backlog

Sprint end date and team deliverable do not change

Finished Work

Sprint Retrospective

ASCEND MANAGEMENT GROUP

Product Backlog

The Product Backlog is a Scrum artifact that serves as the single source of truth for the product's vision and goals. We have been discussing the Product Backlog, and now we can dig in. It's a prioritized list of features, requirements, and tasks that the Development Team will work on to deliver the product. The Product Owner is responsible for creating, maintaining, and refining the Product Backlog, ensuring it remains up-to-date and aligned with stakeholder expectations. I found myself having to hold the Product Owner's hand to ensure the Product backlog is maintained. The Product Backlog contains user stories, epics, and tasks, each with a clear description, acceptance criteria, and estimated effort. Prioritization of the Product Backlog is based on business value, customer needs, and other relevant factors, ensuring the team focuses on delivering the most valuable features first.

The Product Backlog is a dynamic artifact, constantly refined during Backlog refinement, PI planning, and Sprint Planning and updated as new information becomes available. Changes in market conditions, customer feedback, and stakeholder priorities can all impact the Product Backlog, requiring the Product Owner to adapt and adjust the list accordingly. The Development Team collaborates with the Product Owner to ensure they understand the Product Backlog items, providing input on feasibility, complexity, and effort required. This collaboration ensures the team can deliver software that meets customer needs and expectations.

A well-groomed or refined Product Backlog is essential for Scrum success, enabling the team to decide which items to include in the Sprint Backlog. The Product Owner ensures that the top-priority items are clear, concise, and achievable, allowing the team to focus on delivering high-quality software. The

Product Backlog also serves as a communication tool, giving stakeholders visibility into the product's vision and goals. By maintaining a comprehensive and up-to-date Product Backlog, the Product Owner can ensure that the team delivers software that meets customer needs and drives business success. You are a rockstar of a scrum master if you stay on top of your product owner (pause) and confirm and verify that the product backlog has 2 to 3 sprints worth of refined stories. Earn your keep and keep this on your radar as a scrum master.

The Product Backlog is a Scrum artifact that guides the Development Team's work. By prioritizing and refining the Product Backlog, the Product Owner ensures that the team delivers software that meets customer needs and drives business value. The Product Backlog's dynamic nature allows it to adapt to changing requirements and priorities, ensuring the team remains focused on delivering high-quality software.

Sprint Backlog

Sprint Backlog is a Scrum artifact that outlines the specific work to be completed during a Sprint. It's a list of prioritized stories selected from the Product Backlog by the Development Team, ensuring they clearly understand the work to be done. The Sprint Backlog includes specific tasks, estimated effort, and responsibility assignments, providing a clear plan for the team to follow. During the Sprint Planning and PI Planning meetings, the team collaborates to create or refine the Sprint Backlog, ensuring everyone understands their roles and responsibilities. The Sprint Backlog is a commitment by the team to deliver the work outlined, and it remains relatively stable throughout the Sprint.

The Sprint Backlog is a tool for the Development Team to manage their work, track progress, and identify potential roadblocks. It's updated daily during the Sprint, reflecting the team's progress and any changes that may have occurred. The Sprint Backlog is not a comprehensive list of all tasks but a focused list of work that can be realistically completed during the Sprint. The team ensures they deliver the most valuable work possible by prioritizing and selecting specific tasks. The Sprint Backlog also helps the team identify dependencies, risks, and potential impediments, allowing them to address these issues proactively.

A well-crafted Sprint Backlog enables the Development Team to work efficiently, effectively, and collaboratively. It provides a clear direction and focus, ensuring everyone achieves the same goals. The Sprint Backlog also facilitates transparency and accountability, allowing stakeholders to track progress and understand the team's commitment. By regularly reviewing and updating the Sprint Backlog, the team can adapt to changes, identify areas for improvement, and optimize their workflow. On a Kanban board during the sprint, you will see that the sprint backlog stories will be moved to the left as the story progresses. The story will start at the Ready stage and then move to IN-Progress when a team member commits to the work. It is done when the story is completed. Below, you will find how I like setting up my Kanban Board. There could be another stage called BLOCKED when a developer encounters an unforeseen dependency.

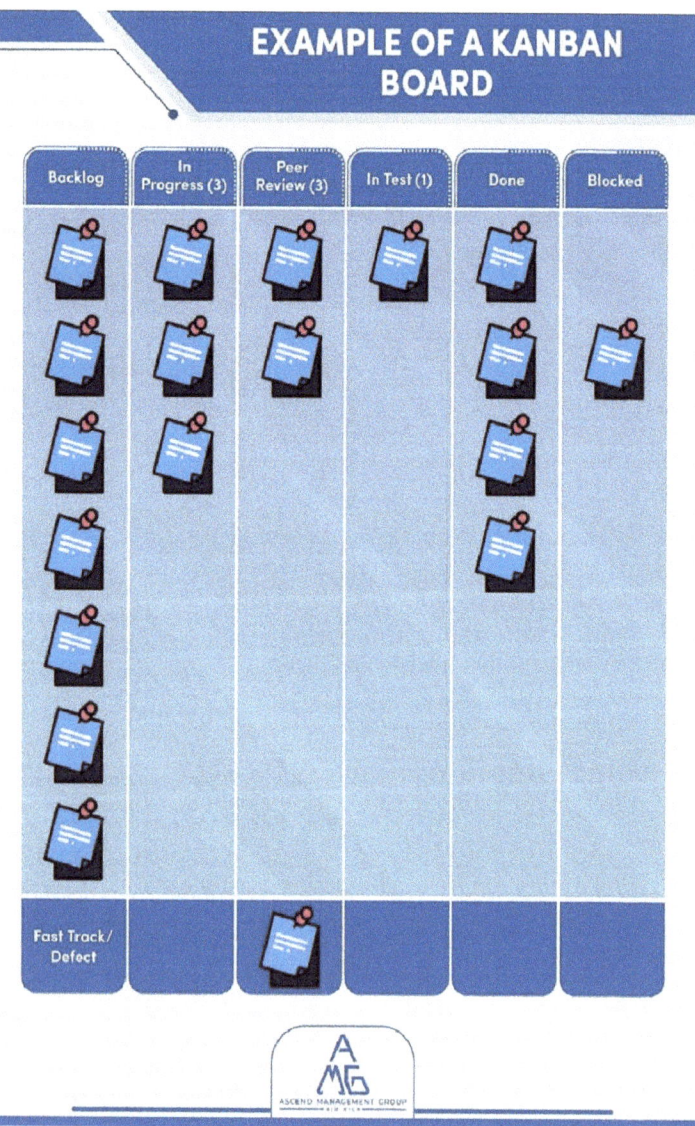

EXAMPLE OF A KANBAN BOARD

Generic Stages:

1. Ready (or To-Do, Backlog, or Queue): Tasks waiting to be started.

2. In-Progress (or WIP, Work-in-Progress): Tasks currently being worked on.

3. Done (or Completed): Tasks completed and verified.

4. Test (Acceptance Criteria performed by Product Owner)

5. Accepted (Verified working as expected by Product Owner).

The Sprint Backlog is a Scrum artifact that outlines the specific work to be completed during a Sprint. It's a commitment by the Development Team to deliver the work outlined, and it serves as a tool for managing work, tracking progress, and identifying potential roadblocks. By prioritizing and selecting specific tasks, the team ensures they're delivering the most valuable work possible, and the Sprint Backlog provides transparency and accountability for stakeholders.

Product Increment

The Product Increment is yet another Scrum artifact representing the sum of all completed work during a Sprint. It's the tangible output of the Sprint, demonstrating the team's progress and commitment to delivering working software. The Product Increment must meet the Definition of Done (DoD), ensuring it's fully functional, tested, and ready for release. During the Sprint Review, the team demonstrates the Product Increment to stakeholders, showcasing the new features and improvements. This artifact provides transparency and accountability, allowing stakeholders to inspect and adapt the product's direction. When showcasing, mentioning issues the team may have encountered is ok. It impresses stakeholders when the team resolves problems and can bring the audience into the development world by overcoming obstacles.

The Product Increment is a crucial aspect of Scrum's iterative and incremental approach, enabling teams to deliver software in short cycles. Each Increment builds upon previous ones, ensuring the product evolves and improves. By delivering a working Product Increment at the end of each Sprint, teams can respond to change and customer feedback more effectively. The Product Increment also serves as a foundation for the next Sprint, allowing teams to plan and prioritize work based on the current state of the product.

A high-quality Product Increment requires collaboration and commitment from the entire Scrum Team. The Development Team works together to complete the work, ensuring it meets the DoD and is fully integrated. The Product Owner provides the Increment aligns with the product vision and goals, while the Scrum Master facilitates the process and removes impediments. By working together, teams can deliver a Product Increment that meets customer needs and drives business value.

In summary, the Product Increment is a vital Scrum artifact that represents the tangible output of a Sprint. It demonstrates the team's progress and commitment to delivering working software, providing transparency and accountability for stakeholders. By delivering a working Product Increment at the end of each Sprint, teams can respond to change and customer feedback more effectively, driving the product's evolution and improvement.

Burn-Down Chart

A burn-down chart visually represents the remaining work in a Sprint, tracking the team's progress toward completing the Sprint goals. It provides a clear picture of the team's velocity and helps identify potential roadblocks or areas for improvement. Show the team the burn-down chart during daily scrum/stand-up. Make it quick, and the team only has 15 minutes.

During the Daily Scrum, the Scrum Master reviews the burn-down chart with the team to track progress and identify areas for adjustment. The Scrum Master explains the current state of the Sprint, highlighting:

"Today is Day 5 of our 10-day Sprint. We've completed 30% of the story points, leaving 70% remaining. Our burn-down chart shows we're slightly behind schedule, indicating we must increase our pace to meet the Sprint goal." Be assertive.

The Scrum Master then facilitates a discussion to identify potential solutions, ensuring the team stays focused on the Sprint objectives. The team has estimated their work honestly. They should do their best to complete work within the estimated time frame and be committed to it.

The burn-down chart is typically presented during various Scrum events:

- Daily Scrum: To track progress and adjust the team's pace.

- Sprint Review: To demonstrate the team's accomplishments and progress toward Sprint goals.

- Sprint Retrospective: To analyze the team's velocity and identify areas for improvement.

Tools for creating burn-down charts include:

- Jira

- Trello

- Asana

- Microsoft Excel

- Google Sheets

- Confluence

Artifacts impacted by the burn-down chart include:

- Sprint Backlog: The burn-down chart reflects the remaining work in the Sprint Backlog.

- Product Backlog: The team's velocity and progress inform Product Backlog prioritization and refinement.

- Increment: The burn-down chart tracks the team's progress toward delivering a potentially shippable Increment.

A burn-down chart can be presented in various formats, including

- Line chart Showing the remaining work over time.

- Bar chart: Comparing actual progress to ideal progress.

- Area chart: Visualizing the remaining work and completed work.

The Scrum Master ensures the burn-down chart is accurate, up-to-date, and easily understandable by the team. By leveraging the burn-down chart, the Scrum Master facilitates data-driven discussions, enabling the team to:

- Identify potential roadblocks

- Adjust their pace

- Improve estimation and planning

- Enhance collaboration and communication

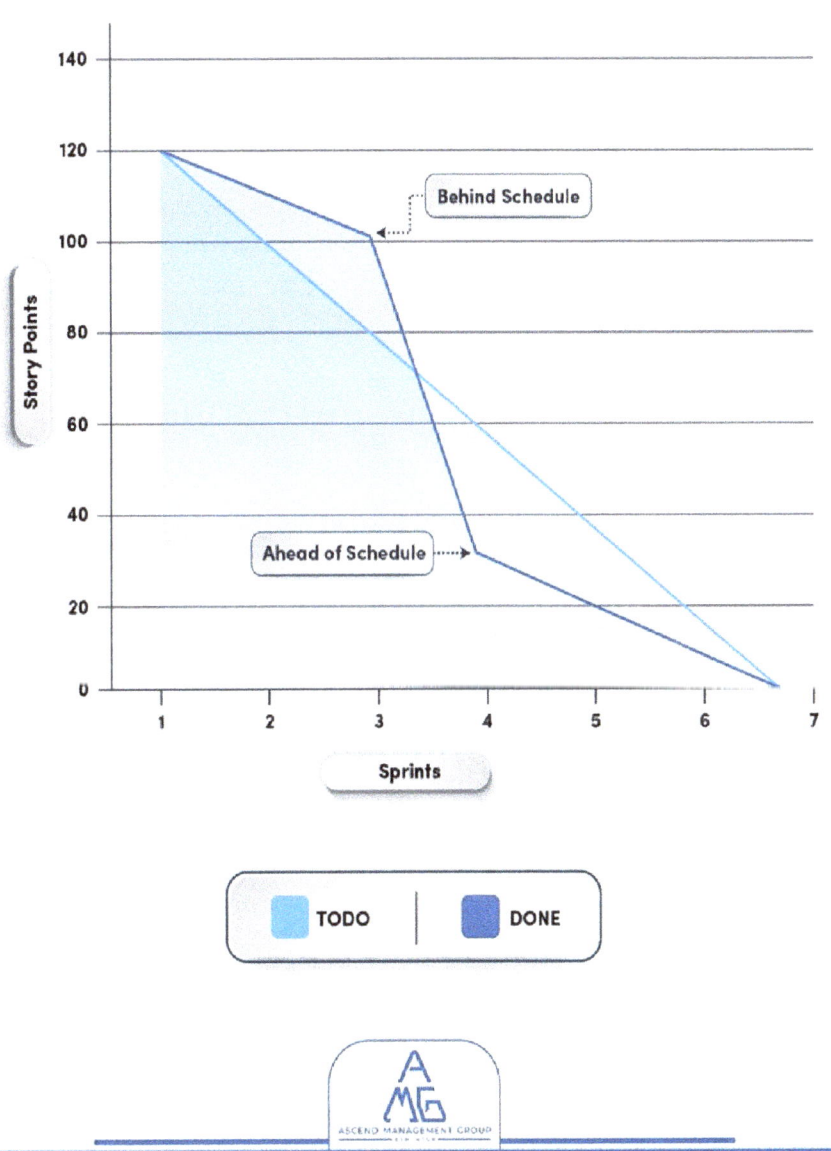

Above is an AMG burn-down chart.

1. A team committed to 120 story points this sprint.
2. Indicates the team's performance. They are starting at 120 story points and working (burning) down to 0 by the end of the sprint. The dark blue spike indicates story points were added, and the team is behind schedule. Deviation from above the lite blue line indicates the team is taking longer than expected on specific stories. If the team is on or under the lite blue line, they are tracking on or ahead of schedule.
3. This is a clear representation of the trajectory they should be on. By the end of the sprint, both lines should meet at ZERO, and the team has hit one of the Sprint Goals.

Based on this diagram, this team needed to complete the stories they committed to. They will move the uncompleted story to the next sprint. Further conservation and examination will take place in Sprint Retrospective. What happened?

In conclusion, the burn-down chart is a powerful tool for Scrum teams to track progress, identify areas for improvement, and ensure successful Sprints. The Scrum Master is crucial in presenting and analyzing the burn-down chart, facilitating team discussions, and driving continuous improvement. Be bold and speak up. Let the team know they need to pick up the pace.

References:

- "Scrum: The Art of Doing Twice the Work in Half the Time" by Jeff Sutherland

- "Agile Project Management with Scrum" by Ken Schwaber

- "Scrum Framework" by Scrum Alliance

- Atlassian Burn-down

Product Road Map

The Product Roadmap outlines the product's vision, goals, and key features over a specific period. It serves as a guiding light for the development team, stakeholders, and customers, ensuring everyone is aligned and working towards the same objectives.

The Product Owner is primarily responsible for creating and maintaining the Product Roadmap. They work closely with stakeholders, including customers, business leaders, and team members, to gather input and feedback. The Product Owner's role is to define the product vision, prioritize features, and ensure the roadmap aligns with business goals. If the Product Owner fails to build or suggest a Product Road map, the Scrum should mention it during PI Planning, Sprint Planning, or Backlog Refinement.

The Development Team plays a vital role in shaping the Product Roadmap. They provide technical insights, feasibility feedback, and estimation guidance to ensure the roadmap is realistic and achievable. The team's input helps the Product Owner prioritize features based on complexity, risk, and resource requirements. Usually, only the Lead Developer is needed to assist with the Product Road Map. Try to avoid bothering the entire team with these items. The team needs to be busy with their commitment.

Stakeholders, including business leaders, customers, and end-users, contribute valuable input to the Product Roadmap. They share market trends, customer needs, and business objectives, helping the Product Owner refine the vision and goals. Stakeholders also provide feedback on the roadmap, ensuring it meets their expectations and requirements. A Scrum Master should schedule this meeting.

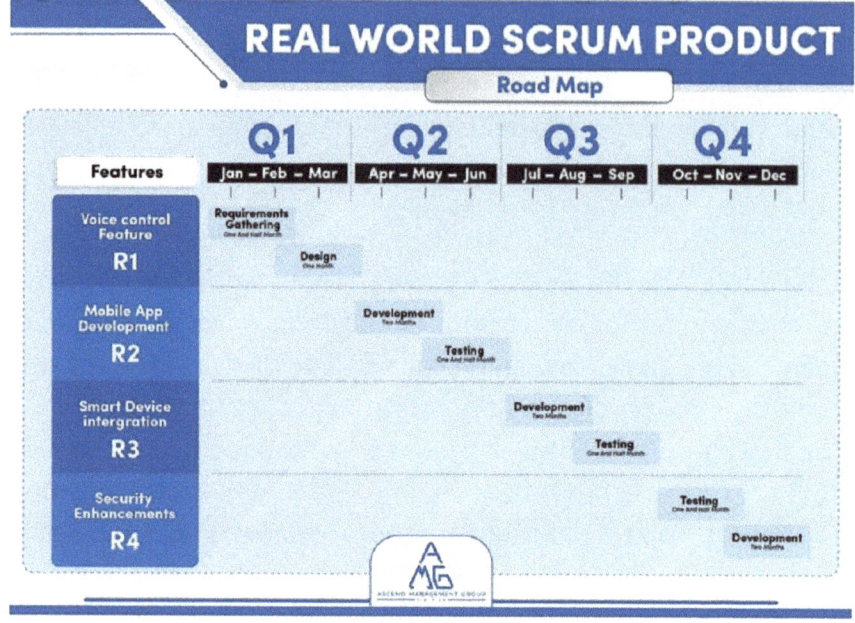

Of course, the Scrum Master facilitates collaboration between the Product Owner, Development Team, and stakeholders. They ensure the Product Roadmap creation process follows Scrum principles and framework. The Scrum Master also guides the team in maintaining a flexible and adaptable roadmap, allowing for changes in requirements or market conditions.

Other team members who contribute to the Product Roadmap include:

Designers provide input on user experience and interface design.

Quality assurance engineers(software testers) ensure the roadmap considers testing and validation.

Technical writers who develop documentation and user guides aligned with the roadmap.

The Product Roadmap typically includes the product vision and mission statement.

Business goals and objectives.

Key features and requirements.

Release plans and timelines.

Resource allocation and budget.

A well-crafted Product Roadmap provides numerous benefits, including:

Clear direction and alignment.

Prioritized features and requirements.

Realistic timelines and resource allocation.

Adaptability to changing market conditions.

Effective communication among stakeholders.

Regular review and updates are essential to maintaining a practical Product Roadmap. The Product Owner should schedule regular roadmap reviews with stakeholders and the Development Team to:

Reflect on progress and accomplishments.

Gather feedback and input.

Refine priorities and adjust timelines.

By collaborating on the Product Roadmap, team members ensure they work towards a shared vision, prioritizing features that deliver value to customers and stakeholders. The Product Roadmap is a dynamic guide navigating the product's evolution and success.

The Scrum Master and the Product Owner

These roles are intricately linked, forming a symbiotic relationship that drives the success of Agile teams. A skilled Scrum Master anticipates the needs of the Product Owner, ensuring seamless collaboration and effective product delivery. This partnership is akin to the dynamic duo of Jared and Richard from the TV show Silicon Valley, where Jared's intuitive understanding of Richard's needs enables the team's success.

A Scrum Master's primary focus is facilitating the Scrum process, removing impediments, and empowering the team. However, to truly excel, they must also develop a deep understanding of the Product Owner's responsibilities and challenges. This includes ensuring the Product Owner has at least two Sprints' worth of well-groomed, high-priority Product Backlog items, meeting the Definition of Ready (DoR) standards. By doing so, the Scrum Master enables the Product Owner to make informed decisions, prioritize effectively, and maintain a steady stream of work for the Development Team. The Scrum master should meet with the PO at least twice weekly outside of regular scrum events. Be proactive and add these meetings to the calendar yourself.

To foster this close relationship, the Scrum Master should:

- Regularly meet with the Product Owner to discuss priorities, goals, and challenges

- Proactively identify potential roadblocks and offer solutions

- Facilitate communication between stakeholders, ensuring the Product Owner's voice is heard

- Guide Product Backlog refinement, ensuring items meet DoR standards

- Monitor progress, identifying areas where the Product Owner may need support

By being attuned to the Product Owner's needs, the Scrum Master can anticipate potential issues and take proactive measures. This might involve:

- Coordinating with stakeholders to clarify requirements

- Facilitating workshops to refine Product Backlog items (Backlog Refinement Events)

- Identifying and mitigating risks

- Ensuring the Development Team understands Product Owner priorities

The Scrum Master is an extension of the Product Owner, amplifying their effectiveness and enabling the team to deliver high-quality software. By mirroring Jared's intuitive understanding of Richard's needs, the Scrum Master can:

- Anticipate information requirements, providing timely updates

- Recognize potential conflicts, resolving them before they escalate

- Streamline communication, ensuring stakeholders are informed

- Foster an environment of trust, empowering the Product Owner to make decisions

This harmonious partnership enables the Product Owner to focus on strategic product decisions while the Scrum Master handles tactical facilitation. As a result, the team benefits from:

- Clear priorities and direction

- Efficient decision-making

- Reduced impediments

- Enhanced collaboration

In Agile environments, the Scrum Master-Product Owner relationship is the foundation! They form an unstoppable duo by cultivating a deep understanding of each other's needs, driving team success, and delivering high-quality software that meets customer needs.

In conclusion, a skilled Scrum Master recognizes the importance of their relationship with the Product Owner. By anticipating needs, ensuring a well-groomed Product Backlog, and fostering open communication, they empower the Product Owner to excel. This partnership, exemplified by Jared and Richard's dynamic in Silicon Valley, is essential for Agile teams to thrive.

The Scrum Master and the RTE (Release Train Engineer)

The Scrum of Scrums is a scaling framework used to coordinate multiple Scrum teams working on complex projects, usually teams dependent on one another. It provides a platform for teams to share knowledge, discuss dependencies, and align their efforts to achieve common goals. In essence, Scrum of Scrums is a meeting of Scrum Masters or team representatives from various Scrum teams.

During Scrum of Scrums, each team representative shares their team's progress, plans, and challenges. This facilitates open communication, fosters collaboration, and enables teams to identify and resolve dependencies. The Scrum Master is vital in facilitating Scrum of Scrums, ensuring that discussions remain focused and productive. Notice in the diagram below the RTE manages the Scrum team on a Program Level Scrum Master on the Team Level.

The Release Train Engineer (RTE) coordinates multiple Scrum teams in large-scale Agile environments. The RTE manages the overall release plan, ensures alignment with organizational goals, and facilitates team communication. The Scrum Master and RTE work closely together to:

Facilitate cross-team collaboration and communication

Identify and resolve dependencies and blockers

Align team goals and objectives with organizational strategies

Develop and implement process improvements

The Scrum Master-RTE relationship is built on trust, open communication, and mutual understanding. The Scrum Master provides insight into team dynamics, progress, and challenges, while the RTE offers guidance on organizational objectives, release planning, and cross-team coordination.

Together, the Scrum Master and RTE:

Develop and refine the release plan,

Identify and prioritize dependencies and blockers,

Coordinate team efforts to achieve release goals,

Monitor progress and adjust plans as needed.

Effective collaboration between Scrum Masters and RTEs enables organizations to:

Scale Agile practices across multiple teams

Improve cross-team communication and collaboration

Enhance release planning and management

Increase productivity and efficiency

In Scrum of Scrums, the RTE participates as a facilitator or observer, providing guidance and oversight. They ensure that discussions align with organizational objectives and release plans.

To facilitate successful Scrum of Scrums, organizations should:

Establish clear objectives and agendas

Define roles and responsibilities for participants

Schedule regular meetings (e.g., daily, weekly, or bi-weekly)

Encourage open communication and collaboration

By leveraging Scrum of Scrums and fostering a robust Scrum Master-RTE relationship, organizations can achieve the following:

Improved cross-team collaboration

Enhanced release planning and management

Increased productivity and efficiency

Better alignment with organizational goals

In conclusion, Scrum of Scrums is a robust framework for coordinating multiple Scrum teams. The Scrum Master-RTE relationship is critical to its success, enabling effective cross-team collaboration, release planning, and alignment with organizational objectives. By understanding and leveraging this relationship, organizations can unlock the full potential of Agile scaling.

Scrum Events (Ceremonies)

S crum events are meetings that occur regularly during a Sprint, providing opportunities for the Scrum Team to inspect and adapt their work. We will go over all of these events in detail. For now, here are The five Scrum events are:

1. Sprint Planning: Occurs at the beginning of each Sprint, where the Development Team and Product Owner collaborate to plan the work for the upcoming Sprint.

2. Daily Scrum: A daily meeting where the Development Team shares their progress, plans their work for the day, and identifies any impediments.

3. Sprint Review: Held at the end of each Sprint, where the Development Team demonstrates the work completed during the Sprint to stakeholders and receives feedback.

4. Sprint Retrospective: This occurs after the Sprint Review, where the Scrum Team reflects on their processes and identifies opportunities for improvement.

5. Backlog Refinement: An ongoing process where the Product Owner and Development Team refine and update the Product Backlog to ensure it remains relevant and aligned with product goals.

These events provide a framework for the Scrum Team to collaborate, inspect, and adapt their work, ensuring they deliver high-quality software that meets customer needs.

Sprint Planning

O ccurs at the beginning of each Sprint, where the Development Team and Product Owner collaborate to plan the work for the upcoming Sprint. Sprint Planning is a critical event in the Scrum framework that sets the stage for a successful Sprint. It's a time-boxed meeting, typically lasting 1-2 hours, where the Scrum Team collaborates to plan the work for the upcoming Sprint. The Scrum Master coaches the team to ensure they understand the objectives and process. Here, we could create a Team Agreement. The meeting is attended by the Development Team, Product Owner, and Scrum Master, with stakeholders invited as needed. While PI planning is for quarterly projects, Sprint planning is usually in 2-week increments. Sprint planning is to refine what was already established in PI Planning.

During Sprint Planning, the Product Owner presents the top-priority items from the Product Backlog, ensuring the team understands the goals and objectives. The team then collaborates to select the items they can realistically complete during the Sprint, considering their capacity and workload. The Scrum Master facilitates the discussion, ensuring the team stays focused and aligned. Scrum Master asserts that the team does not exceed the established workload.

The Product Owner will assign story items to individual team members during this event based on their capacity and skill set. If a team member has stated they can complete up to 8 story points during this sprint, the PO will not assign any more than that. Any more than that, the team member will be set up to fail. In most cases, the team member will request more story items. Allow the team member to finish what is assigned based on capacity before being assigned more. This is the stuff Scrum Masters need to watch out for. Just say no.

The team's responsibilities during Sprint Planning include committing to the work they can complete, identifying dependencies, and ensuring they understand the acceptance criteria. The Product Owner ensures the team understands the Product Backlog items, provides context, and answers questions.

The Scrum Master coaches the team to ensure they're following the Scrum framework and principles. They facilitate the meeting, keep the discussion on track, and ensure the team is progressing towards their goals. The Scrum Master also helps the team identify and mitigate potential impediments.

Sprint planning takes place every two weeks. If the team is planning for a third Sprint, this is where team velocity can be examined. Now, the team knows what they can do, regardless of their workload claims. Velocity is a historical record of story points completed in a sprint. We will talk more about the difference between Capacity and Velocity later.

The Scrum Master should make sure the PO does not exceed team capacity. The Scrum master should confirm with team members that they understand the work that needs to be done. At the end of Sprint Planning, Scrum Master should remind the team of the Sprint Goal and Team Agreement.

Through effective Sprint Planning, the Scrum Team sets themselves up for success, ensuring they're aligned and focused on delivering high-quality software that meets customer needs. The Scrum Master plays a critical role in coaching the team and facilitating the meeting, enabling the team to make informed decisions and commitments. By following the Scrum framework and principles, the team can deliver software that provides real value to customers.

Risks and Dependencies

During Sprint Planning, the Scrum Master promotes risk and dependency identification to the Scrum team. Effective risk management ensures the team delivers high-quality software that meets customer needs. To facilitate this process, the Scrum Master encourages the team to think critically about potential risks and dependencies that may impact the Sprint Goal. In season 1 of Silicon Valley, there was a technical risk of compression algorithm issues. Richard's compression algorithm struggles with video files.

The Scrum Master begins by reviewing the Product Backlog items selected for the Sprint, highlighting the importance of identifying potential risks and dependencies. They explain that risks are uncertain events that, if they occur, can impact the Sprint Goal, while dependencies are critical relationships between tasks or components that require coordination. Dependencies could be encountered within the team or externally. In Silicon Valley, Partnerships: Collaborations with companies like Hooli, EndFrame, and Oracle impact development.

To identify risks, the Scrum Master asks the team to consider questions such as: What could go wrong? What are the potential roadblocks? What are the assumptions we're making? The team discusses each Product Backlog item, exploring potential risks and documenting them for further analysis.

Next, the Scrum Master focuses on dependency identification. They ask the team to examine the relationships between tasks, components, and team members, inquiring: What tasks rely on others? Which components require integration? Are there any external dependencies? By visualizing these dependencies, the team better understands the workflow and potential bottlenecks.

To facilitate effective risk and dependency identification, the Scrum Master employs various techniques. One approach is the "What-If" analysis, where team members imagine potential scenarios that could impact the Sprint Goal. Another technique is the "Pre-Mortem" analysis, where the team assumes the Sprint has failed and identifies possible causes.

The Scrum Master also encourages the team to consider the following:

Historical data: Reviewing past Sprints to identify recurring risks and dependencies.

Technical complexity: Evaluating the technical difficulty of each task.

Team capacity: Assessing the team's workload and availability.

External factors: Considering external influences, such as stakeholder expectations or regulatory changes.

As the team identifies risks and dependencies, the Scrum Master documents and PO prioritize them. This information informs the Sprint plan, enabling the team to develop mitigation strategies and contingency plans.

Throughout the Sprint Planning process, the Scrum Master fosters collaboration and open communication. They encourage team members to share concerns, ask questions, and provide input. By promoting a culture of transparency and shared ownership, the Scrum Master empowers the team to take proactive measures to manage risks and dependencies.

By effectively identifying risks and dependencies during Sprint Planning, the Scrum team can:

Anticipate potential roadblocks

Develop mitigation strategies

Prioritize tasks effectively

Manage stakeholder expectations

Deliver high-quality software that meets customer needs

What is a Spike?

In Scrum, a Spike story is a particular type of user story representing a research-oriented or investigative task to resolve uncertainty, complexity, or risk. Spike stories are used when the team encounters a problem or question that requires exploration before developing. These stories are typically labeled "Spike" or "Research" and have specific characteristics.

A Spike story is created when the team identifies a knowledge gap or uncertainty that blocks progress on a user story or feature. The Spike story is then added to the backlog and prioritized accordingly. The primary goal of a Spike story is to gather information, clarify assumptions, and mitigate risks, enabling the team to make informed decisions and create a more accurate plan.

As a Scrum Master, coaching the team on handling Spike stories involves emphasizing the importance of exploration and discovery. The Scrum Master should encourage the team to identify areas of uncertainty and create Spike stories to address these knowledge gaps. When handling Spike stories, the Scrum Master should guide the team to:

Focus on the specific question or problem being addressed

Define clear objectives and outcomes for the Spike

Establish a time box for the research or investigation

Collaborate and involve relevant stakeholders

Document findings and recommendations

The Scrum Master should also remind the team that Spike stories are not meant to deliver working software but rather to provide valuable insights and information. This distinction helps the team manage expectations and prioritize the Spike story accordingly.

To ensure effective handling of Spike stories, the Scrum Master can facilitate discussions during Sprint Planning, asking questions like: "What specific question are we trying to answer?" or "What risks are we mitigating?" During the Sprint, the Scrum Master can monitor progress and encourage the team to share findings and insights.

By embracing Spike stories and coaching the team on their practical use, the Scrum Master enables them to navigate complex problems, reduce uncertainty, and deliver high-quality products that meet customer needs.

Capacity Planning

During PI and Sprint Planning, team and individual capacity planning are crucial to ensure realistic commitments and successful delivery. The Scrum Master is vital in facilitating capacity planning, enabling the team to make informed decisions. Team capacity planning involves estimating the total work the team can complete during the PI or Sprint, considering factors like velocity, availability, and dependencies.

Individual capacity planning involves understanding each team member's workload, skills, and availability to ensure they're not overcommitted. The Scrum Master uses various tools to capture team capacity, such as capacity planning boards, spreadsheets, or digital tools like Jira or Trello. These tools help visualize the team's capacity, identify potential bottlenecks, and adjust accordingly.

The Scrum Master works closely with the team to estimate their capacity, using historical data, velocity, and expert judgment. They also consider factors like vacations, holidays, and other absences that may impact capacity. By capturing team capacity accurately, the Scrum Master enables the team to make realistic commitments, prioritize work effectively, and deliver high-quality software.

During PI Planning, the Scrum Master facilitates team capacity planning to ensure the team understands their overall capacity for the Program Increment. This involves estimating the total work that can be completed, identifying dependencies, and making necessary adjustments. The Scrum Master uses tools like capacity planning boards or spreadsheets to visualize the team's capacity and facilitate discussion.

In Sprint Planning, the Scrum Master focuses on individual capacity planning, ensuring each team member understands their workload and commitments. They use task boards or digital tools to capture individual capacity, identify potential bottlenecks, and adjust to provide a balanced workload. By considering team and personal capacity, the Scrum Master enables the team to deliver software that meets customer needs while maintaining a sustainable pace.

Effective capacity planning is critical to Scrum's success, enabling teams to make realistic commitments, prioritize work effectively, and deliver high-quality software. The Scrum Master is vital in facilitating capacity planning, using various tools to capture team and individual capacity. Doing so enables the team to work efficiently, adapt to changes, and deliver software that provides real value to customers.

- Developer 1: 8 story points (SP) - they're experienced and can handle complex tasks

- Developer 2: 5 SP - they're relatively new but have shown promise

- Developer 3: 3 SP - they're part-time and only available for 2 days a week

- Developer 4: 8 SP - they're experienced and can handle complex tasks

- Developer 5: 2 SP - they're new and still learning

Team Capacity Planning

To calculate the team's overall capacity, we add up the individual capacities:

8 + 5 + 3 + 8 + 2 = 26 story points

However, we must consider the team's velocity and the average amount of work they can complete during a Sprint. Let's say their velocity is 20 story points per Sprint.

To account for this, we can adjust the team's capacity to 20 story points, a more realistic estimate of what they can achieve during the Sprint.

Fibonacci Estimation

Using Fibonacci numbers, we can estimate the complexity of each task and assign a corresponding story point value:

- Simple tasks: 1-2 SP

- Medium tasks: 3-5 SP

- Complex tasks: 8-13 SP

The team should make a significant attempt to break up the complex task into more minor story points. This will ensure that the task will only take part in the sprint and that any blockers can be addressed during the daily scrum.

Using Fibonacci estimation, we can ensure our estimates are more accurate and consider each task's complexity.

This is a simplified example, and capacity planning may involve more factors and nuances.

Capacity Vs. Velocity

Capacity and Velocity are concepts in Scrum that often need to be understood or clarified. Understanding their differences is essential for effective sprint planning and team performance.

Capacity

We went into Capacity already. It refers to the maximum amount of work a team can handle during a sprint, considering factors like:

- Team size and composition

- Individual work hours and availability

- Skill sets and expertise

- Vacation time and other absences

Capacity is typically measured in hours or days, representing the team's total available workload. Some organizations' scrum team's capacity is measured in 1 story point, equal to 8 hours of work. A team member could hold ten story points of work within a two-week sprint. If a team member takes 2 days of vacation during this sprint, the team member will now be assigned 8 points of work by PO.

Team Members	Capacity	Work Load		
Brian	8	10		
Sonja	10	10		
Kay	10	10		
Lashell	8	10		
Total	36	40		

Brian and Lashell have individual vacation time. The team is now expected to complete 36 story points this sprint.

Velocity measures the work the team completes during a sprint, usually expressed in story points, hours, or work units. Velocity reflects the team's productivity, efficiency, and ability to deliver working software. This helps the team become more predictable. After a few sprints, we now know what the team can do.

Key differences

- Capacity focuses on potential workload, while Velocity measures actual output.

- Capacity is a predictive measure, whereas Velocity is a historical indicator.

- Capacity influences sprint planning, whereas Velocity informs future planning and process improvements.

Mitigating Capacity vs. Velocity issues as a Scrum Master (this will make you powerful)

During Scrum events, a Scrum Master can mitigate Capacity vs. Velocity issues by:

Sprint Planning

1. Ensure the team understands their capacity and velocity.

2. Facilitate realistic goal-setting, considering historical velocity.

3. Encourage the team to commit to achievable objectives.

Daily Scrum

1. Monitor progress and identify potential capacity constraints.

2. Encourage team members to share concerns or obstacles.

3. Facilitate adjustments to ensure alignment with sprint goals.

Sprint Review

1. Analyze velocity and discuss factors influencing it.

2. Celebrate successes and identify areas for improvement.

3. Gather feedback from stakeholders on product increments.

Sprint Retrospective

1. Examine capacity utilization and velocity trends.

2. Discuss process improvements to optimize capacity and velocity.

3. Implement changes to enhance team efficiency and productivity.

Additional Strategies

1. Capacity planning: Use historical data to estimate future capacity.

2. Velocity tracking: Monitor and analyze velocity over time.

3. Team sizing: Adjust team composition to optimize capacity.

4. Cross-training: Develop skills to increase flexibility.

5. Buffering: Allocate contingency time for unexpected tasks.

By understanding the distinction between Capacity and Velocity and actively mitigating potential issues, a Scrum Master enables the team to:

- Set realistic goals

- Optimize workload

- Improve productivity

- Enhance overall Scrum process effectiveness

Effective management of Capacity and Velocity ensures a balanced and sustainable development process, leading to increased team efficiency, productivity, and delivery of high-quality software products.

Sprint Goal

A Sprint Goal is another component of the Scrum framework, providing focus and direction for the Development Team during a Sprint. The Sprint Goal summarizes what the team wants to achieve during the Sprint, aligning with the Product Owner's priorities and the product's overall vision. A skilled Scrum Master plays a vital role in facilitating the creation of a meaningful Sprint Goal.

The Scrum Master typically suggests a Sprint Goal during Sprint Planning after the Product Owner has presented the top-priority Product Backlog items. The Scrum Master's suggestion is based on their understanding of the team's capabilities, the Product Owner's objectives, and the Sprint's overall scope. The goal should be concise, measurable, and achievable within the Sprint timeframe. Sprint Goal could be as simple as a statement or as complex as an Action Item to research a spike story to explore new technologies.

A Sprint Goal can take various forms, including:

- A specific feature or user story

- A collection of related tasks or stories

- An improvement initiative, such as reducing technical debt

- A research or spike story to explore new technologies

Interestingly, a Sprint Goal can also be a 0-point story. This means that the goal's value lies not in its direct contribution to the product's functionality but in its potential to improve the team's processes, knowledge, or overall efficiency. Examples of 0-point Sprint Goals include:

- Improving test automation coverage

- Refactoring legacy code

- Conducting a technical spike to evaluate new tools

Moreover, a Sprint Goal can emerge from action items identified during a Sprint Retrospective. The Retrospective provides an opportunity for the team to reflect on their processes and identify areas for improvement. If the team focuses on a specific improvement initiative, it can become the Sprint Goal for the next Sprint.

For instance, if the team identifies communication breakdowns as a major impediment during the Retrospective, the Sprint Goal might be:

"Improve cross-functional communication by implementing regular team sync-ups and updating the collaboration toolkit."

By setting a clear and achievable Sprint Goal, the Scrum Master helps the team stay focused, motivated, and aligned with the product's vision. Throughout the Sprint, the Scrum Master ensures the team remains committed to the goal, removing impediments and facilitating progress.

The Sprint Goal is a powerful tool for guiding the Development Team's efforts during a Sprint. A skilled Scrum Master suggests a Sprint Goal that aligns with the Product Owner's priorities, the team's capabilities, and the product's vision. Whether a 0-point story or an action item from a Retrospective, the Sprint Goal provides direction and focus, enabling the team to deliver high-quality software that meets customer needs.

Daily Scrum

We have finally kicked off the sprint and are in Daily Scrum. The Daily Scrum, or the Daily Stand-up, is a key event in the Scrum framework. It's a time-boxed meeting, typically 15 minutes, where team members synchronize their work and discuss progress toward the Sprint Goal. The Scrum Master facilitates this meeting, ensuring it remains focused and productive.

Season 2- Episode 1: "Sand Hill Shuffle" - Pied Piper restarts development after Hooli's lawsuit. Let's assume they kicked off a sprint!

The Daily Scrum is a coordination mechanism allowing team members to share their plans for the day, discuss obstacles, and identify dependencies. The Scrum Master needs to create an environment where team members feel comfortable sharing their challenges and concerns. To achieve this, the Scrum Master should encourage active listening, foster open communication, and promote collaboration. Here, I would randomly select a team member to start the conversation. When the team member completes their updates, they will nominate another team member to provide their updates. Doing it this way will keep the team engaged because they don't know when a team member will randomly choose them.

During Daily Scrum, the Scrum Master or Product Owner will update the Sprint Backlog as a Kanban Board to reflect the story transition. Scrum master should remind team members to update the progress of stories before Daily Scrum to save time. Now that's empowerment!

During the Daily Scrum, each team member typically answers three questions:

"What did I work on yesterday?"

"What will I work on today?"

"Are there any impediments or obstacles blocking my progress?"

These questions help team members focus on their tasks, identify potential roadblocks, and prioritize their work. The Scrum Master should pay close attention to the answers, taking note of dependencies, risks, or impediments that may impact the Sprint Goal.

It is critical to discuss dependencies during the daily scrum. Team members should identify any dependencies that may affect their work, such as waiting on input from another team member or relying on external stakeholders. The Scrum Master should help the team visualize these dependencies, ensuring everyone understands the impact on the overall workflow.

To facilitate practical discussion, the Scrum Master may ask additional questions, such as:

"What's the most critical task you need to complete today?"

"How does your work align with the Sprint Goal?"

"Are there any potential risks or blockers that could impact our progress?"

"Have you discussed your dependencies with the relevant team members?"

"What's the estimated time required to complete your task?"

By asking these questions, the Scrum Master encourages team members to think critically about their work, prioritize tasks, and collaborate with colleagues. The Scrum Master should also use this opportunity to remove impediments, provide guidance, and ensure the team remains focused on the Sprint Goal.

A good Scrum Master will listen and identify which team members may not understand the Scrum Framework. The Scrum Master should never embarrass the team member. However, the Scrum Master should approach the team member and schedule a one-on-one coaching session. Make sure the Team member doesn't feel singled out. These are knowledgeable individuals, and they should be respected at all times. Sometimes, their pride will not allow them to express that they don't understand a concept. A good Scrum Master should recognize the shortcomings.

Time-boxing is essential in the Daily Scrum. The Scrum Master must ensure the meeting stays within 15 minutes, keeping discussions concise and relevant. This time constraint encourages team members to prioritize updates and focus on critical information. Scrum Master may respectfully interrupt long conversations and request to continue offline.

To maintain a productive Daily Scrum, the Scrum Master should:

Monitor the time and keep discussions on track

Encourage active listening and open communication

Foster collaboration and teamwork

Identify and address dependencies and impediments

Ensure alignment with the Sprint Goal

By facilitating an effective Daily Scrum, the Scrum Master enables the team to work collaboratively, adapt to changes, and deliver high-quality software that meets customer needs.

The Daily Scrum is a component of the Scrum framework. The Scrum Master will guide and facilitate this event, ensuring it remains focused, productive, and aligned with the Sprint Goal. By asking the right questions, identifying dependencies, and removing impediments, the Scrum Master empowers the team to deliver software efficiently and effectively.

Daily Scrum Task Management

A Scrum Master plays a vital role in facilitating Daily Scrum and ensuring the smooth progression of Sprint Backlog items. Task management boards are essential in this process, visually representing work items and their status. The board is a central hub for the team to track progress, identify impediments, and align their efforts.

During Daily Scrum, the Scrum Master begins by reviewing the task management board (usually JIRA) to ensure all team members understand the work items. This visual check-in helps identify potential blockers or bottlenecks, allowing the team to address them promptly. The Scrum Master then asks each team member to share their progress, plans, and impediments, updating the board accordingly.

The task management board typically consists of columns representing different stages of work: Ready, In Progress, and Done. The Ready column holds items waiting to be started, while In Progress contains items currently being worked on. The Done column displays items finished and meeting acceptance criteria. Some boards also include a Blocked column to highlight items hindered by impediments.

As team members complete tasks, the Scrum Master moves items from Ready to In Progress when work begins. The board is updated as team members progress, and items are moved to Done when acceptance criteria are met. This visual workflow enables the team to track velocity and Sprint progress, identifying areas for improvement.

The Scrum Master's role is to update the board and facilitate collaboration and communication among team members. Using the task management board, the Scrum Master encourages active participation, ensures alignment with Sprint goals, and identifies potential roadblocks.

Effective use of task management boards requires the Scrum Master to ensure the board accurately reflects the team's work. This involves keeping the board up-to-date, organized, and free from clutter. Clear and concise language should be used for work items, and Work-In-Progress (WIP) limits should be established to prevent overcommitting.

Digital task management boards, such as Jira, Trello, or Asana, offer flexibility and accessibility for distributed teams. These platforms provide real-time updates, notifications, and customizable workflows. Physical boards, like sticky notes or whiteboards, provide a tactile experience and face-to-face collaboration.

Some teams opt for a hybrid approach, combining physical and digital boards to leverage both benefits, for instance, using a physical board for Daily Scrum and a digital board for remote team members or stakeholders.

In addition to facilitating Daily Scrum, task management boards help the Scrum Master track Sprint progress and identify trends. By analyzing the board, the Scrum Master can pinpoint bottlenecks, adjust WIP limits, and refine the team's workflow.

During Sprint Review and Retrospective, the task management board is a valuable resource for evaluating team performance and process improvements. The Scrum Master can review the board to identify successful patterns and areas for growth, incorporating these insights into future Sprints.

In conclusion, task management boards are a powerful tool for Scrum Masters to facilitate Daily Scrum and track Sprint Backlog items. By leveraging these boards, Scrum Masters can enhance team collaboration, visualize work, and drive successful Sprints. Effective use of task management boards requires attention to detail, clear communication, and a commitment to continuous improvement.

Team Contribution to Daily Scrum

The development team comprises developers, testers, designers, and other professionals working on the product.

The Scrum Master is responsible for facilitating the meeting, ensuring the Scrum framework is followed, and removing impediments.

The Product Owner may attend to clarify Product Backlog items, answer questions, and ensure alignment with the product vision.

During the Daily Scrum, each Development Team member shares their:

Progress since the previous meeting

Plan for the current day

Potential blockers or impediments hindering their progress

The Scrum Master's primary role is to facilitate the meeting, ensuring it remains focused and productive. They:

Encourage active participation and open communication

Monitor time, keeping discussions concise

Identify and document potential blockers or impediments

Guide Scrum processes and principles

To capture blockers or impediments, the Scrum Master takes meeting minute notes. These notes should be concise, clear, and actionable. The Scrum Master records:

Blockers or impediments mentioned by team members

Action items assigned to team members or stakeholders

Decisions made during the meeting

Follow-up tasks or next steps

For example:

"Luther mentioned difficulty integrating the new API due to unclear documentation. Action item: Scrum Master will coordinate with the API owner for clarification."

"Team discussed challenges with testing environment setup. Decision: Allocate 2 hours today for environment configuration."

After the Daily Scrum, the Scrum Master reviews and analyzes the captured data to:

Identify recurring blockers or impediments

Recognize patterns or trends in team progress

Inform the Product Owner of potential risks or delays

Develop strategies to mitigate impediments

The Scrum Master uses this data to:

Remove impediments by coordinating with stakeholders or team members

Facilitate communication between team members and stakeholders

Update the Scrum Board or project management tools

Inform retrospective discussions for process improvements

By capturing and analyzing data from the Daily Scrum, the Scrum Master enables the team to:

Address potential roadblocks proactively

Improve collaboration and communication

Enhance productivity and efficiency

Refine Scrum processes for better outcomes

In addition, the Scrum Master may share meeting notes and action items with stakeholders and the Product Owner, ensuring transparency and accountability.

To maintain effective Daily Scrum meetings, the Scrum Master should:

Distribute meeting notes and action items promptly

Establish a clear format for meeting notes

Regularly review and update the Scrum Board

Encourage team members to update their task status

By facilitating productive Daily Scrum meetings and capturing essential data, the Scrum Master empowers the Development Team to deliver high-quality software efficiently.

The Daily Scrum is an event where essential team members discuss progress, plans, and potential obstacles. The Scrum Master is a master note taker and plays a massive role in facilitating meetings, capturing notes, and analyzing data to remove impediments and improve team productivity. By leveraging this data, the Scrum Master enables the team to deliver software efficiently and effectively. I told you I would repeat concepts to hammer important concepts home.

Sprint Review / Demo

The Sprint Review/Demo is an interactive event in the Scrum framework, marking the conclusion of a Sprint. This meeting allows the Development Team to showcase their accomplishments, receive feedback, and demonstrate the working software they've developed.

Use this time to brag and showcase the ups and downs of the iteration. Crack jokes, have fun, and be confident in your team's capabilities. Play some upbeat music while the attendees are entering the room. Create a vibe of positive energy. Yes, this is a serious scrum event, but don't let that keep you from controlling the atmosphere. You want to make people want to be a part of the conversation.

A scrum master should always be in a state of showing value in the presence of colleagues and team members. We are more than just facilitators. We are also leaders. Give 110% every chance you get. Make yourself known, and earn your keep. The following is Pure Gold. You can thank me later.

Pre-Sprint Review Meeting -

Before the Sprint Review/Demo, the Scrum Master convenes a team meeting to:

Discuss the agenda and objectives

Assign presentation responsibilities to team members

Review the Sprint Backlog and ensure accuracy

Coordinate logistics and technical setup

This preparatory meeting ensures the team is well-prepared and that the Sprint Review/Demo proceeds smoothly.

Sprint Review/Demo Agenda-

The Sprint Review/Demo typically follows this agenda:

1. Introduction and welcome (Scrum Master)

2. Review of Sprint Goal, Team Capacity, and Team Velocity (Scrum Master)

3. Presentation of completed User Stories (Development Team)

4. Discussion of incomplete User Stories (Development Team)

5. Stakeholder feedback and Q&A

6. Review of action items and next steps

Scrum Master's PowerPoint Presentation-

The Scrum Master prepares a PowerPoint presentation covering the following:

Sprint Goal: A summary of the Sprint's objectives

Team Capacity: An overview of the team's available resources and workload

Team Velocity: Historical data on the team's productivity and progress

Sprint Backlog: A review of the User Stories planned for the Sprint

Example slides:

Slide 1: Sprint Goal

"Sprint Goal: Enhance User Authentication and Authorization"

Slide 2: Team Capacity

"Team Capacity: 120 hours available for development"

Slide 3: Team Velocity

"Team Velocity: Average 20 User Story points completed per Sprint"

Slide 4: Sprint Backlog

"Sprint Backlog: 10 User Stories, prioritized by Product Owner"

Development Team Presentation-

The Development Team showcases the completed User Stories, highlighting:

Key features and functionality

Technical accomplishments and challenges

Testing and quality assurance efforts

Team members demonstrate the working software, providing stakeholders with hands-on experience.

Discussion of Incomplete User Stories-

The Development Team discusses User Stories that were not completed, explaining:

Reasons for incomplete work (e.g., technical difficulties, scope changes)

Lessons learned and areas for improvement

Plans for completing remaining work

This open discussion fosters transparency and accountability.

Stakeholder Feedback and Q&A-

Stakeholders provide feedback on the presented work, asking questions and:

Clarifying requirements and expectations

Offering suggestions for future improvements

Acknowledging team achievements

Action Items and Next Steps-

The Scrum Master summarizes action items, next steps, and:

Outstanding tasks or defects

Upcoming Sprint priorities

Follow-up meetings or discussions

The Sprint Review/Demo concludes with a clear understanding of the team's accomplishments, areas for improvement, and future directions.

Best Practices-

To ensure a successful Sprint Review/Demo:

Schedule the meeting well in advance

Invite relevant stakeholders and ensure attendance

Prepare a clear and concise presentation

Assign presentation responsibilities to team members

Leave time for Q&A and feedback

Following these guidelines, the Scrum Master facilitates an effective Sprint Review/Demo, showcasing the team's progress and fostering stakeholder collaboration.

Sprint Retrospective

A Sprint Retrospective is a team-building event in the Scrum framework, held at the end of each Sprint, where the team reflects on their processes, identifies areas for improvement, and implements changes to enhance productivity and quality. This meeting provides an opportunity for the team to examine what went well, what didn't, and what can be improved in the next Sprint.

The primary objective of the Sprint Retrospective is to continuously improve the team's processes, ensuring they remain aligned with the Scrum framework and the organization's goals. During this meeting, the team discusses their experiences, shares insights, and identifies growth opportunities. Retrospective focuses on processes, not individuals, and encourages open and honest communication.

I like to use a Mural board. I would provide a link to the team member a day before Sprint Retrospective. We will save time if the board is almost populated. The columns would include what went well, What we can improve on, and Action items. Give the team 7 minutes to fill in one column while mild music plays. Then, we would discuss the team feedback for 10 minutes and then move to the next column. The goal is to get the team talking and out of their shell. Always be looking to extract action items from their input. When Action items are present, start assigning them to team members. Also, at the beginning of every retro, I would add, "This is a safe space. Everyone here is equal. If you need something from me or have a critique of your scrum master, please let me know. I have tough skin. "When assigning action items, follow up with team members during Daily Scrum to verify action items are being resolved.

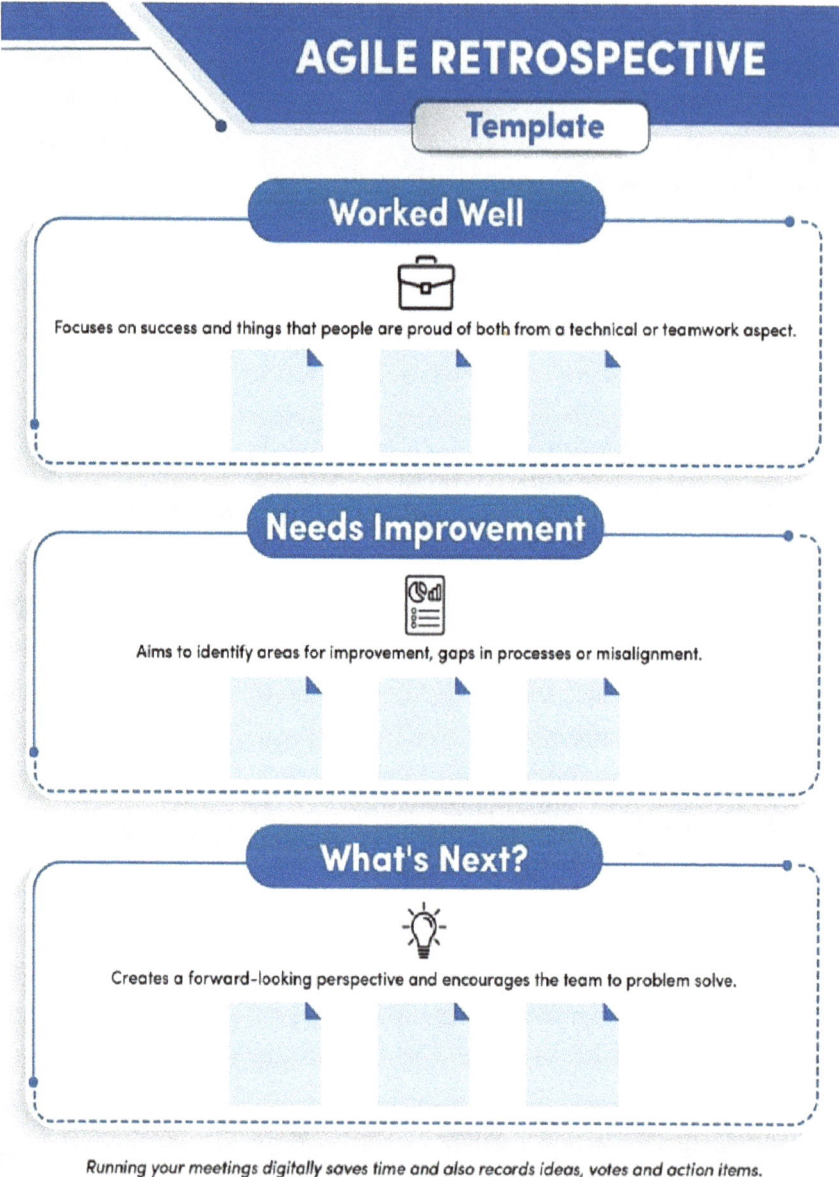

AGILE RETROSPECTIVE

Template

Worked Well

Focuses on success and things that people are proud of both from a technical or teamwork aspect.

Needs Improvement

Aims to identify areas for improvement, gaps in processes or misalignment.

What's Next?

Creates a forward-looking perspective and encourages the team to problem solve.

Running your meetings digitally saves time and also records ideas, votes and action items.

ASCEND MANAGEMENT GROUP

The Scrum Master plays a vital role in facilitating the Sprint Retrospective. Their primary contribution is to create a safe and constructive environment, ensuring all team members feel comfortable sharing their thoughts and opinions. The Scrum Master guides the discussion, keeps the meeting focused, and helps the team identify actionable improvements. They also ensure that the team's suggestions are feasible, measurable, and aligned with the Scrum framework.

Attendees for the Sprint Retrospective typically include:

The Development Team is responsible for implementing process changes.

The Product Owner will provide input on product-related aspects and ensure alignment with product goals.

The Scrum Master facilitates the meeting and ensures Scrum principles are followed.

Optional attendees may include:

Stakeholders, to provide valuable insights and perspectives.

Team leaders manage to support the team's decisions and provide guidance.

During the Sprint Retrospective, the team discusses various aspects, such as:

Communication and collaboration within the team.

Efficiency of meetings and processes.

Technical debt and coding standards.

Testing and quality assurance.

Product backlog management.

The Scrum Master encourages the team to identify and prioritize improvements that are specific, measurable, achievable, relevant, and time-bound (SMART). The team then selects the most critical improvement for the next sprint.

The Sprint Retrospective concludes with a clear plan for implementing changes, assigned responsibilities, and a review of the action items. The Scrum Master ensures that the agreed-upon improvements are incorporated into the team's processes and monitored during the next Sprint.

By conducting regular Sprint Retrospectives, teams can:

Enhance collaboration and communication.

Improve processes and efficiency.

Increase productivity and quality.

Boost morale and job satisfaction.

The Sprint Retrospective team-building event in the Scrum framework enables teams to reflect, improve, and adapt to changing requirements. The Scrum Master's facilitation and guidance ensure a productive and constructive discussion, leading to actionable improvements and continuous growth.

Sprint Retrospect Deep-Dive

During a Sprint Retrospective, the Scrum team examines various artifacts to identify areas for improvement and optimize their processes. The primary artifacts under review are the Sprint Backlog, Product Backlog, Increment, and Burn-down Chart.

The Sprint Backlog is scrutinized to assess the team's ability to deliver the planned work. The team evaluates which items were completed, partially, or left undone and why. They analyze the estimated effort versus actual effort, identifying discrepancies and opportunities to refine estimation techniques.

The Product Backlog is also examined to ensure it remains relevant, up-to-date, and aligned with the product vision. The team reviews the backlog's clarity, prioritization, and refinement, making adjustments to improve the product's overall direction.

The Increment, representing the sum of all Product Backlog items completed during the Sprint, is inspected to verify its quality and adherence to the Definition of Done. The team assesses whether the Increment meets the required standards and identifies any defects or technical debt that need attention.

The Burn-down Chart, tracking the remaining work hours or story points throughout the Sprint, provides valuable insights into the team's velocity and progress. The team analyzes the chart to identify trends, patterns, or anomalies and adjusts their estimation and planning processes accordingly.

Other artifacts that may be examined during the Sprint Retrospective include:

The Definition of Done to ensure it remains relevant and effective in providing quality.

The Team's Working Agreements are to verify they are still relevant and valuable.

The product owner's prioritization decisions are used to assess their impact on Sprint's objectives.

The Development Team's technical practices include testing, coding standards, and continuous integration.

By examining these artifacts, the Scrum team gains a comprehensive understanding of their strengths, weaknesses, and areas for improvement. They can identify the need to be more efficient in their processes and workflows.

Opportunities to improve estimation and planning.

Ways to enhance collaboration and communication.

Methods to increase productivity and quality.

The insights from examining these artifacts enable the team to create actionable improvements for the next Sprint. The Scrum Master facilitates this process, ensuring the team stays focused on constructive changes that align with the Scrum framework.

The Sprint Retrospective concludes with a clear plan for implementing improvements, assigned responsibilities, and a review of the action items. The Scrum Master ensures that the agreed-upon enhancements are incorporated into the team's processes and monitored during the next Sprint.

By regularly examining Scrum artifacts in the Sprint Retrospective, teams can refine their processes, enhance collaboration, and improve overall productivity and quality. This continuous improvement mindset is essential to Scrum's success, enabling teams to adapt to changing requirements and deliver high-value products.

Sprint Retrospective Task Management

To conduct a productive Sprint Retrospective, a Scrum Master employs various tools to facilitate discussion, identify improvements, and capture action items. Here are the standard tools used:

Collaboration and Idea Generation Tools:

- Digital whiteboards like Mural, Google Jamboard, or Microsoft Whiteboard

- Online sticky notes like Sticky Notes, Trello, or Asana

- Mind mapping tools like MindMeister or Coggle

Virtual Meeting Tools:

- Video conferencing platforms like Zoom, Google Meet, or Skype

- Screen sharing and recording tools like Loom or ScreenFlow

Task Management Tools:

- Jira, Trello, or Asana for capturing and assigning action items

- Microsoft Planner, Google Tasks, or (link unavailable) for task management

- Confluence or Notion for note-taking and knowledge management

Retrospective Facilitation Tools:

- Retrium, a dedicated Sprint Retrospective tool

- Scrum Genius, a Scrum-focused collaboration platform

- FunRetro, a gamified Retrospective tool

Other Tools:

- Survey and feedback tools like SurveyMonkey or Google Forms

- Collaboration platforms like Slack or Microsoft Teams

During the Sprint Retrospective, the Scrum Master uses these tools to:

- Facilitate discussion and idea generation

- Identify and prioritize areas for improvement

- Capture action items and assign responsibilities

- Track progress and follow up on improvements

Task management tools are essential for capturing action items, assigning tasks, and tracking progress. The Scrum Master ensures that:

- Action items are clear, concise, and measurable

- Tasks are assigned to specific team members

- Due dates and priorities are established

- Progress is tracked and reviewed

By leveraging these tools, Scrum Masters can facilitate effective Sprint Retrospectives, drive continuous improvement, and enhance team collaboration and productivity.

Backlog Refinement

Backlog refinement, also known as grooming, is an essential process in Scrum that ensures the Product Backlog is up-to-date, relevant, and ready for the Development Team to work on. The Product Owner is responsible for conducting backlog refinement, with the Scrum Master providing guidance and support.

The Product Owner begins by reviewing the Product Backlog, identifying items that require refinement or clarification. They assess the backlog's overall health, look for duplicate or outdated items, and remove or update them as necessary. The Product Owner also considers the product vision, roadmap, and stakeholder feedback to ensure alignment.

During refinement, the Product Owner breaks down prominent user stories into smaller, more manageable tasks. They define acceptance criteria, ensuring the Development Team understands the requirements and can deliver the desired outcome. The Product Owner also estimates the effort required for each item, using techniques like story points or hours.

The Scrum Master is vital in supporting the Product Owner during backlog refinement. They ensure the Product Owner stays focused on the tasks, guiding Scrum principles and best practices. The Scrum Master helps the Product Owner maintain a clear and concise Product Backlog, free from ambiguity.

To facilitate refinement, the Scrum Master may ask open-ended questions, such as:

"What is the primary goal of this user story?"

"How does this item align with the product vision?"

"What are the key acceptance criteria for this feature?"

"How will we measure the success of this item?"

By asking these questions, the Scrum Master encourages the Product Owner to think critically about the Product Backlog, ensuring it remains relevant and practical.

The Scrum Master also helps the Product Owner prioritize the Product Backlog, using techniques like MoSCoW prioritization or Kano analysis. They facilitate discussions with stakeholders to clarify requirements and expectations.

To stay on task, the Scrum Master respectfully reminds the Product Owner of the refinement goals and time constraints. They ensure the Product Owner:

Stays focused on the current refinement session's objectives

It avoids scope creep and maintains a clear product vision

Involve stakeholders and team members as necessary

Reviews and updates the Product Backlog regularly

Through effective backlog refinement, the Product Owner and Scrum Master collaboration ensures:

A clear and concise Product Backlog

Well-defined user stories with acceptance criteria

Accurate effort estimation

Prioritized items aligned with the product vision

Regular refinement sessions, ideally held during the Sprint or immediately after, maintain the Product Backlog's integrity. The Scrum Master facilitates these sessions, ensuring the Product Owner stays on track.

By conducting regular backlog refinement, the Product Owner and Scrum Master enable the Development Team to:

Work efficiently on well-defined tasks

Deliver high-quality products meeting customer needs

Adapt quickly to changing requirements

In conclusion, backlog refinement is used to maintain a healthy Product Backlog. The Product Owner, with the Scrum Master's guidance, ensures the backlog remains relevant, up-to-date, and ready for the Development Team. Effective collaboration between the Product Owner and Scrum Master enables successful backlog refinement, driving the team toward delivering high-value products.

Congratulations!

Congratulations on completing Real World Scrum! This achievement marks a significant milestone in your Agile journey, empowering you to excel as a Scrum Master and beyond. The knowledge and insights gained will substantially boost your confidence in facilitating flexible Scrum events, coaching teams to self-organize, and delivering high-quality products.

As a Scrum Master, you're better equipped to navigate complex projects, foster a culture of transparency and accountability, and drive continuous improvement and learning. Your ability to remove impediments, resolve conflicts, and encourage open communication and feedback will significantly enhance team collaboration and productivity.

However, the benefits of Real World Scrum extend far beyond formal Scrum Master roles. These concepts can be applied to personal projects, non-Scrum teams, leadership roles, and entrepreneurial ventures to improve collaboration, adaptability, and decision-making. You can leverage this expertise to drive iterative progress, customer satisfaction, and meaningful change.

With your newfound knowledge, you'll enhance your professional reputation, expand your network, and stay adaptable in an ever-changing work environment. Embracing the Scrum mindset will help you celebrate teamwork, encourage continuous learning, and deliver exceptional results. Congratulations again on completing Real World Scrum! You're now poised to make a lasting impact with Agile methodologies.

This accomplishment will transform your project management, teamwork, and leadership approach.

Practice Exam

Exam Name: Certified Scrum Master (CSM)

Total Questions: 142 Q&As

QUESTION 1

What is the maximum time the team should spend in the daily scrum?

A. As long as it takes

B. 1 hour

C. 45 minutes

D. 15 minutes

E. 15 minutes, proportionally less for shorter Sprints

Correct Answer: D

QUESTION 2

Please select which statement is the most accurate:

A. Agile Development is an implementation of Scrum

B. Scrum is an implementation of agile development

C. Agile Development and Scrum are synonyms for the same methodology

D. Agile Development and Scrum are contrasting methodologies

Correct Answer: B

QUESTION 3

Which of the following is not a Product Owner's responsibility?

A. Running the daily scrum meeting

B. Working with stakeholders to determine and detail product features

C. Gathering requirements for Product Backlog items

D. Inspecting work at Sprint Review

Correct Answer: A

QUESTION 4

How should items in the Product Backlog be ordered?

A. Alphabetically first and then by list order in the Product Backlog

B. Grouped by business features first and then chronologically by date of original business request

C. Prioritized by business importance first. The items that result in the most significant ROI, must be prioritized first;

D. Chronologically by date of original business request first and then by list order in the Product Backlog

Correct Answer: C

QUESTION 5

Which of the following is a role in the Scrum framework?

A. Database Admin

B. Development Team

C. QA Tester

D. Senior Developer

Correct Answer: B

QUESTION 6

Does the Scrum Framework encompass rules or guidelines for documentation?

A. True

B. False

Correct Answer: B

QUESTION 7

The individual, detailed pieces of work that are needed to convert a product backlog item into a working software component or solution are called:

A. User Stories

B. Use cases

C. Line items

D. Tasks

Correct Answer: D

QUESTION 8

Why does Scrum prevent product owners from changing product backlog items being worked on during the Sprint?

A. The development team cannot meet their Sprint commitment to complete work if requirements are changing

B. A Sprint cycle is not enough time for senior management to review and approve changes

C. This forces Product Owners to focus on what is essential for the team to develop

D. The development team must be able to limit the Product Owner's authority

Correct Answer: A

QUESTION 9

Which of the following is not a Scrum artifact?

A. User Stories

B. Sprint Backlog

C. Product Backlog

D. Incremento de Software

Correct Answer: A

QUESTION 10

You are the new Scrum Master at a company that is currently doing RUP in three-month iterations. When switching from RUP to Scrum, your current task is to define how long the Sprint cycle should be. In what units of time should you define the sprint cycle?

A. A fixed amount of months

B. A fixed amount of weeks, excluding holidays

C. A fixed amount of days

D. A fixed amount of hours

Correct Answer: C

QUESTION 11

Which of the following statements best explains what Sprint means in Scrum?

A. A sprint is a specific amount of days for a team to test and resolve any issues before product release or shipment

B. A sprint is a specific number of days for a team to work sustainably to finish select work.

C. A sprint is an agreed-upon time for team members to select individual items from the product backlog to work on.

D. A sprint is a specific amount of days for a team to work as many hours as needed to finish assigned work

Correct Answer: B

QUESTION 12

Who can change the priority of items in the backlog at any time?

A. The Team; Product

B. The Product Owner(s); Sprint

C. The Product Owner(s); Product

D. The Scrum Master; Sprint

Correct Answer: C

QUESTION 13

Which of the following is not a Scrum cycle activity?

A. Sprint retrospective

B. Daily scrum

C. Weekly inspection

D. Sprint planning

Correct Answer: C

QUESTION 14

Which of the following statements best describes Product Backlog items?

A. Undefined or poorly defined Product Backlog items should be placed on the Product Backlog with a low-priority

B. All Product Backlog items result from a(n) analysis, requirements, and design phase (s).

 C. Undefined or poorly defined Product Backlog items should be kept out from the Product Backlog until sufficient detail is known.

D. Every Product Backlog item, whether low priority or high priority, should possess sufficient detail for the Team to complete in a Sprint.

Correct Answer: A

QUESTION 15

_____constitute the Sprint Backlog and are often estimated in hours?

A. User Stories

B. Use Cases

C. Features

D. Tasks

Correct Answer: D

QUESTION 16

Under what circumstances should separate Product Backlogs be maintained?

A. There are several Product Owners for one product. Each product owner should have a product backlog.

B. multiple teams are working on independent products. Each unique combination of team and product should have an independent Product Backlog

C. The same team is developing multiple product features.

D. multiple teams are working on the components of the same product. Each team should have an independent Product Backlog

Correct Answer: B

QUESTION 17

Who determines whether the development team has been assigned enough work in a Sprint?

A. The Development Team

B. The Product Owner

C. The Product Owner and the Scrum Master

D. The Scrum Master

Correct Answer: A

QUESTION 18

Which of the following is not a Product Owner's responsibility?

A. Maintaining the Product Backlog with current information

B. Working with stakeholders to determine and detail product features

C. Assigning tasks to team members

D. Prioritizing the Product Backlog

Correct Answer: C

QUESTION 19

Which of the following activities do not occur at the end of the Sprint?

A. Software development

B. Release Deployment

C. Sprint review meeting

D. Quality assurance testing

Correct Answer: ABD

QUESTION 20

What does the Scrum Development Team attempt to develop every Sprint?

A. A product that is ready for customer delivery

B. A completed Sprint Backlog

C. A product that is ready for QA and QC testing

D. A product increment that is potentially ready for customer delivery

Correct Answer: D

QUESTION 21

A _____ is created during the first half of the Sprint planning meeting, and a_____ is created during the second half of the Sprint planning meeting.

A. Sprint Backlog, collection of tasks

B. Product Backlog, collection of tasks

C. Sprint Goal, Sprint Backlog

D. Product Backlog, Sprint Backlog

Correct Answer: C

QUESTION 22

How many sections does the Sprint planning meeting consist of?

A. 4

B. 3

C. 2

D. 1

Correct Answer: C

QUESTION 23

Please select which of the following statements are true

A. The Product Owner itemizes which Product Backlog items are done and which Product Backlog items are not done during Sprint Review

B. The Product Owner demonstrates potentially shippable product features and components during the Sprint Review

C. The Scrum Master provides a report of what happened during the Sprint

D. The Development Team demonstrates potentially shippable product features and components during the Sprint Review

E. Feedback from stakeholders during the Sprint Review may result in additional Product Backlog Items

Correct Answer: ABE

QUESTION 24

What is the maximum duration of each Sprint planning meeting section?

A. 1 hour

B. 30 minutes

C. 4 hours

D. 2 hours

E. 15 minutes

Correct Answer: C

QUESTION 25

From the activities given, which is the last step in sequence of the Scrum framework?

A. Daily scrum

B. Sprint retrospective

C. Sprint review

D. Sprint planning

Correct Answer: B

QUESTION 26

Which of the following is not a Scrum Master responsibility?

A. Establish priorities together with the product owner for Product Backlog items

B. Preventing Senior Management from shifting team priorities

C. Empowering the team

D. Socializing scrum throughout the organization

Correct Answer: A

QUESTION 27

Which of the following is reflected in a Sprint Burndown Chart?

A. Team Members Name

B. Number of Product Backlog Items Completed

C. Number of Tasks Remaining

D. Work Hours Remaining

Correct Answer: D

QUESTION 28

How many hours per day should a person on a Scrum team work?

A. A sustainable pace, usually from 7-8 hours per day.

B. An "ideal day" measures only when they are productive.

C. However many hours are needed to get the work done.

D. 14 hours.

Correct Answer: A

QUESTION 29

According to Scrum, the amount of time a team takes to plan Sprint activities is expressed in what unit of time?

A. Weeks

B. Days

C. Hours

D. Minutes

Correct Answer: C

QUESTION 30

You are the Scrum Master, and your Development Team of 6 members has completed six Sprints with the following information:

Sprint 1: 10 points

Sprint 2: 11 points

Sprint 3: 15 points

Sprint 4: 14 points

Sprint 5: 15 points

Sprint 6: 10 points

The remaining story points for product development total 42. What is the approximate number of sprints required to complete product development?

A. 6

B. 5

C. 4

D. 3

Correct Answer: C

QUESTION 31

Under what circumstances should the Product Backlog be reprioritized?

A. The Scrum Master should reprioritize the Product Backlog only at the end of a new Sprint B. The Scrum Master should reprioritize the Product Backlog only at the beginning of a new Sprint

C. The Team should reprioritize the Product Backlog only at the end of a newSprint.

 D. The Product Owner should reprioritize the Product Backlog whenever new information is learned

Correct Answer: D

QUESTION 32

How could the team and other stakeholders know if a product backlog item is done?

A. They should ask the member's development team

B. They should compare what was done, against the definition of Done established by the Scrum Team

C. Ask the Product Owner

D. Ask the Manager

Correct Answer: C

QUESTION 33

What is the primary objective of the daily scrum?

A. To share with the team what each member has completed in the Sprint, what each member will work on next, and to report progress roadblocks

B. To give a status report to the Product Owner on what each member has completed in the Sprint and what each member will work on next, and to report progress roadblocks.

C. Discuss work details with the team since every team member must attend the meeting.

D. Give a status report to the Scrum Master on what each member has completed in the Sprint and what each member will work on next, and report progress roadblocks.

Correct Answer: A

QUESTION 34

Which statement best describes what it means for an activity to be time-boxed?

A. The activity must take place on a particular date

B. The activity must start at a particular time

C. There is a maximum time limit for the activity

D. There is a recommended amount of time for the activity

Correct Answer: C

QUESTION 35

Which statement below best describes the primary objective of the Sprint Review?

A. The primary objective of the Sprint Review is to demo the Sprint work for Senior Management B. The primary objective of the Sprint Review is to demo the Sprint work and to receive feedback from the Product Owner(s) on the work completed in the Sprint

C. The primary objective of the Sprint Review is to demo the Sprint work and to receive feedback from the Scrum Master on the work completed in the Sprint

D. The primary objective of the Sprint Review is to demo the Sprint work and to recommend ways to work better in the Sprint.

Correct Answer: B

QUESTION 36

You are the Scrum Master; the first Sprint will be completed in 5 days. You are creating a meeting invite for the Sprint Review to demo the items completed in the Sprint. Who should you invite as a required attendee to the Sprint Review?

1. Product Owner(s)

2. Development Team

3. Business Users

A. 1, 2, and 3

B. 1 and 2 only

C. The entire company

D. 1 only

Correct Answer: B

QUESTION 37

You are the Scrum Master. The Sprint will be completed in two days. Each day of the Sprint is equivalent to 8 hours. The team has enough time to complete all tasks except for three in the remaining 16 hours. Of these three tasks, two tasks (a total of 6 hours) are required to complete one Product Backlog item, and one task (an estimate of 2 hours) is required to complete another Product Backlog item. How should the development team handle the remaining three tasks?

A. The development team should negotiate with the Product Owner on the definition of"done." B. The development team should work the extra 8 hours to complete their commitment to the Product Owner

C. The development team should place the two Product Backlog items back onto the Product Backlog

D. The development team should keep the three tasks on the Sprint Backlog for the next Sprint and complete those tasks first

Correct Answer: C

QUESTION 38

Which statement below best describes the primary objective of the Sprint Retrospective?

A. The primary objective of the Sprint Retrospective is to identify what went wrong or hindered the Sprint

B. The primary objective of the Sprint Retrospective is to provide feedback to the Product Owner(s).

C. The primary objective of the Sprint Retrospective is to recommend ways to work better in the Sprint

Correct Answer: C

QUESTION 39

Which of the following is not reflected in a Sprint Burndown Chart?

A. Total Days in Sprint

B. Number of Tasks Remaining

C. Day of Sprint

D. Work Hours Remaining

Correct Answer: B

QUESTION 40

What artifact shows actual versus planned progress?

A. What artifact shows actual versus planned progress?

B. Burndown Chart

C. Task Breakdown

Correct Answer: B

QUESTION 41

Which of the following is NOT part of the Sprint?

A. The product is released to customers after each Sprint

B. The principal goal for a Sprint is to produce release-quality increments in functionality

C. Releases usually incorporate the result of multiple Sprints

D. Occur at times dictated by customer and business needs

Correct Answer: A

QUESTION 42

What is the maximum time a sprint retrospective should take?

A. 1 hour

B. 1 and a half hour

C. 3 hours for a 30-day Sprint

Correct Answer: C

QUESTION 43

What happens when all committed items (requirements) are not completed at the end of the Sprint?

A. The Sprint duration is extended

B. The tasks are determined to be unnecessary

C. They return to the product backlog

D. None of the above

Correct Answer: C

QUESTION 44

The most encouraged time of day to hold a Scrum Daily Meeting is

A. A beginning of the day

B. Immediately after lunch

C. 4:30 PM

D. 7:00 PM

Correct Answer: A

QUESTION 45

Is Scrum Master a "management" position?

A. Yes

B. No

Correct Answer: A

QUESTION 46

Who is on the Scrum Team?

A. Project Manager

B. Project Owner

C. Product Owner

D. Development Team

E. Manager

F. CEO

G. Scrum Master

Correct Answer: CDG

QUESTION 47

What is the recommended size for a Development Team?

A. 6, +3 or -3

B. 9

C. 6

D. 7, +2 or -2

Correct Answer: A

QUESTION 48

Who is required to attend the Daily Scrum?

A. Scrum Master

B. Development Team

C. Development Team and Product Owner

D. Development Team and Scrum Master

Correct Answer: B

QUESTION 49

On a new Scrum Team, the Development Team tells the Scrum Master that they don't need retrospectives. Which answer is correct:

A. Discuss with the product owner

B. Start doing retrospectives

C. None of the above

Correct Answer: B

QUESTION 50

The Product Backlog is maintained by:

A. The Scrum Master

B. The Development Team

C. The Product Owner

D. The Product Owner and Scrum Master

Correct Answer: C

QUESTION 51

What is Scrum?

A. A framework within which people can address complex adaptive problems while productively and creatively delivering products of the highest possible value

B. It's not a Agile Framework

C. Scrum is a complete process of developing software

D. None of the above

Correct Answer: A

QUESTION 52

The correct sequence of events in using the Scrum framework is as follows:

A. Sprint Planning, Sprint, Sprint Retrospective, Daily Scrum, and Sprint Review

B. Sprint Planning, Sprint, Daily Scrum, Sprint Review, and Sprint Retrospective

C. Sprint Planning, Sprint, Sprint Retrospective, Daily Scrum, and Sprint Review

D. Sprint Planning, Daily Scrum, Sprint, Sprint Review, and Sprint Retrospective

Correct Answer: B

QUESTION 53

Who has the authority to cancel a Sprint?

A. The team members

B. The Scrum Master

C. The Product Owner

D. The Project Manager

Correct Answer: C

QUESTION 54

Who defines the Sprint Backlog scope?

A. Product Owner

B. Development Team

C. Scrum Master

D. Stakeholders

Correct Answer: B

QUESTION 55

What is the significant difference between Product Backlog and Sprint Backlog?

A. The Product Backlog is equal to the Sprint Backlog

B. The Product Backlog is a subset of the SprintBacklog

C. The Sprint Backlog is a subset of the product backlog

D. The Sprint Backlog is owned by the Product Owner

Correct Answer: C

QUESTION 56

As the Sprint planning progresses, the workload has grown beyond the development team's capacity. Which action makes the most sense for the Team?

A. Work overtime for the Sprint

B. Collaborate with the Product Owner and potentially remove or change items

C. Cancel the Sprint

D. Star the Sprint and recruit additional team members

Correct Answer: B

QUESTION 57

What does the Sprint Backlog consist of?

A. User Stories, only.

B. Use Cases

C. Selected Backlog Items and Tasks

D. Test cases

Correct Answer: C

QUESTION 58

What happens when the Sprint is canceled?

A. The Scrum Team disbands immediately

B. The complete Sprint Backlog is put back into the Product Backlog

C. The completed Sprint Backlog items are evaluated for a release, and incomplete items are discarded

D. The completed Sprint Backlog items are evaluated for a release, and incomplete items are put back into the Product Backlog

Correct Answer: D

QUESTION 59

What is the Release Burndown?

A. A graph indicating what has been completed by Scrum Team

B. A measure of the remaining Product Backlog across the time of a release plan C. What has been completed by the Scrum Team to date

D. The work remaining to be completed by the Product Owner

Correct Answer: B

QUESTION 60

Who is ultimately responsible for the Product Backlog item estimates?

A. The Development Team

B. Scrum Master

C. Stakeholders

D. Project Owner

Correct Answer: A

QUESTION 61

More than one Scrum Team is working on a single project or release. How should the Product Backlog be arranged?

A. A separate Product Backlog is constructed for each Scrum Team. All of the increments are integrated at the end in an integration Sprint

B. All Scrum Teams work from a common Product Backlog and integrate their work every sprint

C. Only one Scrum Team should work on the Scrum project.

D. Scrum Teams should have their separate Product Backlogs

Correct Answer: B

QUESTION 62

When many Scrum Teams are working on a project, what best describes the definition of "done"?

A. All teams must use the exact definition

B. Each Team defines and uses its own

C. Each Team uses its own but must make it clear to all other Teams

D. It depends

Correct Answer: A

QUESTION 63

When many Scrum Teams work on the same product, should their increments be integrated every Sprint?

A. No, that is far too hard

B. No, each Scrum Team stands alone

C. Yes, but only the Scrum Teams whose work has dependencies

D. Yes, otherwise Product Owners may not be able to inspect what is done accurately

Correct Answer: D

QUESTION 64

What is the primary responsibility of the Scrum Master?

A. To Prioritize the Product Backlog

B. To remove any impediments the Development Team encounters during their work C. To work with the Product Owner to develop the Product Backlog

D. To manage the Development Team

Correct Answer: B

QUESTION 65

When should the Product Owner ship or implement a Sprint increment?

A. At the end of every Sprint

B. When the Team feels it is done with every Sprint

C. Whenever the increment is free of defects

D. When it makes sense

Correct Answer: A

QUESTION 66

The Sprint Backlog is owned by?

A. The Scrum Master

B. The Product Owner

C. The Development Team

D. The Scrum Master and Development Team

Correct Answer: C

QUESTION 67

Which objectives are covered as part of Sprint Planning?

A. Understand what functionality the Product Owner desires within the next Sprint and determine how to do it

B. Updating the scope of the release with all Sprints, end dates, and costs

C. Reviewing current functionality that binds the software solution

D. Recalculating empirical velocity, adjusting team capacity accordingly, and projecting end dates

Correct Answer: A

QUESTION 68

The Development Team should have all the skills needed to:

A. Complete the project as estimated when the date and cost are committed to the Product Owner.

B. Turn the Product Backlog, which it selects, into an increment of potentially shippable product functionality.

C. Do all of the development work but not the types of testing that require specialized testing, tools, and environments.

Correct Answer: B

QUESTION 69

Who determines when updating the Sprint Backlog during a Sprint is appropriate?

A. The Project Manager

B. The Scrum Team

C. The Development Team

D. The Product Owner

Correct Answer: C

QUESTION 70

Which of these may a Development Team deliver at the end of a Sprint (choose 2)?

A. A single document, if that is what the Product Owner asked for

B. An increment of software with minor known bugs in it

C. Failing unit tests to identify acceptance tests for the next Sprint

D. An increment of working software that is "done."

Correct Answer: BD

QUESTION 71

Which three activities will a Product Owner likely engage in during a Sprint?

A. Run the daily Scrum

B. Answer questions from the Development Team about items in the current Sprint

C. Update the Sprint burndown chart

D. Work with the stakeholders

E. Prioritize the Development Team's activities.

F. Provide feedback

Correct Answer: BDF

QUESTION 72

Development Team members volunteer to own a Sprint Backlog item:

A. During the Daily Scrum

B. Whenever a team member can accommodate more work

C. Never. All Sprint Backlog Items are "owned" by the entire Development Team, even though an individual team member may do each one

D. At the Sprint planning meeting

Correct Answer: C

QUESTION 73

Which two are properties of the Daily Scrum? (Choose 2)

A. It is fifteen minutes or less in duration.

B. The team lead facilitates it.

C. It consists of the Scrum Master asking the Team members the three questions.

D. Its location and time should remain constant.

Correct Answer: AD

QUESTION 74

What is the primary way a Scrum Master keeps a Development Team working at its highest level of productivity?

A. By ensuring the meetings start and end at the proper time

B. By facilitating Development Team decisions and removing impediments

C. By preventing changes to the Backlog once the Sprint begins

D. By keeping high-value features high in the product backlog

Correct Answer: B

QUESTION 75

Which statement best describes Scrum?

A. A framework within which complex products in complex environments are developed B. A defined and predictive process conforming to Scientific Management C's principles. A cookbook that describes best practices for software development

D. A complete methodology that defines how to develop software

Correct Answer: A

QUESTION 76

Which of the following might the Scrum Team discuss during a Sprint Retrospective?

A. Methods of communication

B. The way the Scrum Team does Sprint Planning

C. Skills needed to improve the Development Team's ability to deliver

D. Its Definition of Done

E. All of the above

Correct Answer: E

QUESTION 77

Which three questions are answered by all Development Team members at the Daily Scrum?

A. What work am I going to do today?

B. Why were you late?

C. What impediments are in the way of my accomplishing my work?

D. What work did I do yesterday?

E. How is the Sprint proceeding?

Correct Answer:ACD

QUESTION 78

When is the Sprint Backlog created?

A. At the beginning of the project

B. Before the Sprint Planning meeting

C. During the Sprint

D. During the Sprint Planning meeting

Correct Answer: D

QUESTION 79

The Sprint Goal is selected before the Sprint Backlog is created.

A. True

B. False

Correct Answer: A

QUESTION 80

Who should know the most about the progress toward a business objective or a release and be able to explain the alternatives most clearly?

A. The Product Owner

B. The Scrum Master

C. The Project Manager

D. The Development Team

Correct Answer: A

QUESTION 81

Upon what type of process control is Scrum-based?

A. Hybrid

B. Defined

C. Complex

D. Empirical

Correct Answer: D

QUESTION 82

What is the maximum time Scrum recommends the team spend in the daily scrum (daily standup)?

A. Fifteen minutes

B. Thirty minutes

C. One hour

D. Four hours

E. As long as it takes

Correct Answer: A

QUESTION 83

Which topics should be discussed in the Sprint Review?

A. the process

B. coding practices

C. all of the above

D. Sprint results

Correct Answer: D

QUESTION 84

What is the Time-box for the Sprint Retrospective?

A. As long as required.

B. 1 hour.

C. 2 hours.

D. 3 hours.

Correct Answer: D

QUESTION 85

Who must conform to the definition of done?

A. The Product Owner

B. The development team

C. The Scrum team

D. The QA department

Correct Answer: C

QUESTION 86

Which statement is an incorrect assessment of the Product Owner?

A. The Product Owner plays a dual role: Product Owner and Scrum Master.

B. The Product Owner is the only person responsible for the product backlog.

C. The Product Owner prioritizes the Product Backlog

D. The Product Owner is one person, not a committee.

Correct Answer: A

QUESTION 87

When should the Product Owner ship or implement a Sprint increment?

A. At the end of every Sprint.

B. When the Team feels it is done with every Sprint.

C. Whenever the increment is free of defects.

D. When it makes sense.

Correct Answer: A

QUESTION 88

When does Scrum team membership change?

A.   When team members have an attitude problem.

B. As needed, while taking into account short-term reduction in productivity.

C. Never, because it reduces productivity.

D. Whenever management tells the Scrum team.

Correct Answer: B

QUESTION 89

How much work must a Scrum Team do to a Product Backlog it selects for a Sprint?

A. As much work as the Team can fit into a Sprint.

B. All the analysis, design, development, testing, and documentation work.

C. The best amount of work the Team can do given that it is usually impossible for QA to finish all the testing needed to prove it can be shipped.

D. As much work as it has told the Product Owner will be done for every Product Backlog item it selects.

Correct Answer: D

QUESTION 90

When is new work or further decomposition of work added to the Sprint Backlog during a Sprint?

A. When the Product Owner identifies a new work.

B. As soon as possible after they are identified.

C. During the Daily Scrum after the Development Team approves them.

D. When the Scrum Master has time to enter them.

Correct Answer: B

QUESTION 91

Which of the following are the leading Scrum roles in a Scrum Team?

A. Product Owner and Customers.

B. Development Team, Product Owner, and Scrum Master.

C. ScrumMaster, Customers, Product Owners, Stakeholders, Developers.

D. Team, Users, and Competitors.

Correct Answer: B

QUESTION 92

What is the best term to define the function of the Scrum Master?

A. Customer

B. Developer

C. Servant Leader

D. Stakeholder

Correct Answer: C

QUESTION 93

When is a Sprint over?

A. When all Sprint Backlog items meet their definition of "done."

B. When all the tasks are completed.

C. When the Product Owner says it is done.

D. When the time box expires

Correct Answer: D

QUESTION 94

What part of the Sprint Backlog is used for the Sprint burndown chart?

A. The percentage of work completed by each Team member.

B. The number of Product Backlog items completed by all the Team members.

C. The actual time spent on each task by each team member.

D. Each team member requires the remaining time to complete each task.

Correct Answer: D

QUESTION 95

The Sprint Backlog is owned by?

A. The Product Owner.

B. The Scrum Master.

C. The Stakeholders.

D. The Development Team.

Correct Answer: D

QUESTION 96

Which objectives are covered as part of Sprint Planning?

A. Updating the release scope with all Sprints, end dates, and costs.

B. Recalculating empirical velocity, adjusting team capacity accordingly, and projecting end dates.

C. Reviewing current functionality that binds the software solution.

D. Understand what functionality the Product Owner desires within the next Sprint and determine how to do it.

Correct Answer: D

QUESTION 97

When should the Sprint Retrospective be held?

A. At the end of the last Sprint in a project or release.

B. At the beginning of each Sprint.

C. Only when the Scrum team determines it needs one.

D. At the end of each Sprint.

Correct Answer: D

QUESTION 98

Assuming a 2-week Sprint, What is the Time-box for the Sprint Review?

A. 2 hours at the end of every sprint.

B. 15 minutes.

C. However long is needed.

D. 4 hours.

Correct Answer: A

QUESTION 99

Which statement best describes the Sprint Review?

A. It is used to build Team spirit.

B. It is a time allocated to judge the validity of the project.

C. It allows stakeholders to inspect the product increments and progress to date and to provide feedback

D. It is a review of the Team's activities during the Sprint.

Correct Answer: C

QUESTION 100

Who is ultimately responsible for the Product Backlog item estimates?

A. ScrumMaster.

B. Product Owner.

C. Stakeholders

D. Development Team

Correct Answer: D

QUESTION 101

What is the Release Burndown?

A. A graph indicating what has been completed by the Scrum Team.

B. What has been completed by the Scrum Team to date?

C. The work remaining to be completed by the Product Owner.

D. A measure of the remaining Product Backlog across the time of a release plan.

Correct Answer: D

QUESTION 102

What happens when the Sprint is canceled?

A. The Scrum Team disbands immediately.

B. The complete Sprint Backlog is put back into the Product Backlog.

C. The completed Sprint Backlog items are evaluated for release, and incomplete items are discarded.

D. The completed Sprint Backlog items are evaluated for a release, and incomplete items are put back into the Product Backlog.

Correct Answer: D

QUESTION 103

More than one Scrum Team is working on a single project or release. How should the Product Backlog be arranged?

A. A separate Product Backlog is constructed for each Scrum Team. All of the increments are integrated at the end in an integration Sprint

B. All Scrum Teams work from a common Product Backlog and integrate their work every sprint

C. Only one Scrum Team should work on the Scrum project.

D. Scrum Teams should have their separate Product Backlogs.

Correct Answer: B

QUESTION 104

When many Scrum Teams are working on a project, what best describes the definition of "done"?

A. Each Team defines and uses its own.

B. Each Team uses its own but must make it clear to all other Teams.

C. All teams must use the exact definition.

D. It depends.

Correct Answer: C

QUESTION 105

What's the Scrum Team's definition of "Done"?

A. Whatever the ScrumMaster wants it to be.

B. Whatever the Product Owner wants it to be.

C. Whatever the Stakeholders want it to be.

D. Whatever the Scrum Team defines "done" to be

Correct Answer: D

QUESTION 106

What is the primary responsibility of the ScrumMaster?

A. To Prioritize the Product Backlog.

B. To manage the Scrum Team.

C. To work with the Product Owner to develop the Product Backlog.

D. To remove any impediments the Development Team encounters during their work.

Correct Answer: D

QUESTION 107

A Sprint can be canceled by whom?

A. ScrumMaster

B. Sprint Team

C. Management

D. Product Owner

Correct Answer: D

QUESTION 108

How much time should be dedicated to the Sprint Planning Activity for a one-month Sprint?

A. 8 Hours.
B. Whatever time is needed.
C. 1 Month
D. 4 hours.

Correct Answer: A

QUESTION 109

A properly functioning Scrum team will have at least one Release Sprint and may well have several

A. Truc

B. False

Correct Answer: B

QUESTION 110

The correct sequence of events in using the Scrum framework is as follows:

A. Sprint 0, Sprint Planning, Sprint, Sprint Retrospective, Daily Scrum, and Sprint Review.
B. Sprint Planning, Sprint, Daily Scrum, Sprint Review, and Sprint Retrospective.

C. Sprint Planning, Sprint, Retrospective, Daily Scrum, and Sprint Review.

D. Sprint Planning, Daily Scrum, Sprint, Sprint Review, and Sprint Retrospective.

Correct Answer: B

QUESTION 111

When is a Product Backlog item considered complete?

A. When all defined tasks are complete.
B. When QA reports that it passes all acceptance criteria.
C. When it adheres to the definition of "done."
D. At the end of the Sprint.

Correct Answer: C

QUESTION 112

Which statement is an incorrect assessment of the Development Team?

A. The Development Team is self-organizing.

B. The Development Team is responsible for the Sprint Backlog.

C. The Development Team is cross-functional

D. The Development Team comprises fifteen members with various sets of skills.

 Correct Answer: D

QUESTION 113

What does it mean for a Development Team to be cross-functional?

A. The Development Team is a virtual team drawing from separate teams of business analysts, architects, developers, and testers.

B. The Development Team includes cross-skilled individuals who can contribute to doing what is necessary to deliver an increment of software.

C. Developers on the Development Team work closely with business analysts, architects, developers, and testers who are not on the team.

D. The Development Team includes developers, business analysts, architects, developers, and testers.

Correct Answer: B

QUESTION 114

What is the recommended size for a Development Team (within the Scrum Team)

A. 6 plus or minus 3

B. 3 plus or minus 1

C. 15 plus or minus 3

D. 9 plus or minus 2

Correct Answer: A

QUESTION 115

What is the significant difference between Product Backlog and Sprint Backlog?

A. The Product Backlog is equal to the Sprint Backlog

B. The Product Backlog is a subset of the Sprint Backlog.

C. The Sprint Backlog is a subset of the Product Backlog.

D. The Product Owner owns the Sprint Backlog.

Correct Answer: C

QUESTION 116

The maximum duration of the Sprint is highly recommended to be.

A. 5 days.

B. 10 days.

C. 15 days.

D. Less than a month.

Correct Answer: D

QUESTION 117

The workload has grown beyond the team's capacity as the Sprint planning progresses. Which action makes the most sense for the Team?

A. Work overtime for the Sprint

B. Collaborate with the Product Owner and potentially remove or change items

C. Cancel the Sprint

D. Star the Sprint and recruit additional team members

Correct Answer: B

QUESTION 118

What does it mean to say that an event is time-boxed?

A. The event must take at least a minimum amount of time.

B. The event must happen at a given time.

C. The event must happen at a set time.

D. The event can take no more than a maximum amount of time.

Correct Answer: D

QUESTION 119

What is the role of Management in Scrum?

A. To monitor the Development Team's productivity.

B. To continually monitor staffing levels of the Development Team.

C. Management supports the Product Owner with insights and information into high-value product and system capabilities. Management supports the Scrum Master to cause organizational change that fosters empiricism, self-organization, bottom-up intelligence, and intelligent software release.

D. To identify and remove people who aren't working hard enough.

Correct Answer: C

QUESTION 120

The Development Team should have all the skills needed to:

A. Turn the Product Backlog it selects into an increment of potentially shippable product functionality

B. Complete the project as estimated when the date and cost are committed to the Product Owner

C. Do all of the development work but not the types of testing that require specialized testing, tools, and environments

Correct Answer: A

QUESTION 121

When a Development Team determines that it has over-committed itself for a Sprint, who has to be present when reviewing and adjusting the Sprint work selected?

A. The Scrum Master, Project Manager, and Development Team.

B. The Development Team

C. The Product Owner and Development Team.

D. The Product Owner and all stakeholders.

Correct Answer: C

QUESTION 122

Who is responsible for updating the work estimates during a Sprint?

A. The Scrum Master.

B. The Development Team.

C. The Product Owner

D. The most junior member of the Team.

Correct Answer: B

QUESTION 123

How much work must a Development Team do to a Product Backlog item it selects for a Sprint?

A. As much as it has told the Product Owner that will be done for every Product Backlog item it selects in conformance with the definition of done

B. As much as it can fit into the sprint.

C. Analysis, design, programming, testing, and documentation

D. The best it can do given that it is usually impossible for QA to finish all of the testing that is needed to prove shippability

Correct Answer: A

QUESTION 124

The CEO asks the Development Team to add a "very important" item to the current Sprint. What should the Development Team do?

A. Add the item to the current Sprint and drop an item of equal size.

B. Add the item to the next Sprint.

C. Inform the Product Owner so they can work with the CEO.

D. Add the item to the current Sprint without any adjustments.

Correct Answer: C

QUESTION 125

The Development Team should not be interrupted during the Sprint. The work it selects for the Sprint should remain the same. The Sprint Goal should remain intact. These attributes of a Sprint foster creativity, quality, and productivity. Based on this, which of the following is false?

A. As a decomposition of the selected Product Backlog Items, the Sprint Backlog changes and may grow as the work emerges.

B. The Sprint Backlog and its contents are fully formulated in the Sprint Planning meeting and do not change during the Sprint.

C. The Product Owner can help clarify or optimize the Sprint when the Development Team asks.

D. The Development Team may work with the Product Owner to remove or add work if it finds it has more or less capacity than expected

Correct Answer: B

QUESTION 126

Which two (2) things does the Development Team not do during the first Sprint?

A. Develop a plan for the rest of the project.

B. Nail down the complete architecture and infrastructure.

C. Develop and deliver at least one piece of functionality.

D. Deliver an increment of potentially shippable functionality.

Correct Answer: AB

QUESTION 127

What is the primary way a Scrum Master keeps a Development Team working at its highest level of productivity?

A. By keeping high-value features high in the product backlog.

B. By ensuring the meetings start and end at the proper time.

C. By facilitating Development Team decisions and removing impediments.

D. By preventing changes to the Backlog once the Sprint begins.

Correct Answer: C

QUESTION 128

What is the timebox for the complete Sprint Planning meeting?

A. 8 hours for a monthly Sprint, proportionately less for shorter sprints

B. 4 horas.

C. Monthly..

D. Whenever it is done.

Correct Answer: A

QUESTION 129

The product increment must be released to production or shipped to customers at the end of each Sprint.

A. True

B. False

Correct Answer: B

QUESTION 130

What is the maximum length of a Sprint?

A. Not so long that the risk is unacceptable to the Product Owner.

B. Not so long that other business events can't be readily synchronized with the development work.

C. No more than one calendar month.

D. All of these answers are correct.

Correct Answer: D

QUESTION 131

Scrum does not have a role called "project manager."

A. True

B. False

Correct Answer: A

QUESTION 132

Who has the last say on the order of the Product Backlog?

A. The CEO

B. The Development Team

C. The Stakeholders

D. The Product Owner

E. The Scrum Master

Correct Answer: D

QUESTION 133

The Product Backlog is ordered by:

A. Safer items at the top to riskier items at the bottom.

B. Least valuable items at the top to most valuable at the bottom.

C. Small items are at the top, and large items are at the bottom.

D. Items are randomly arranged

Whatever is deemed most appropriate by the product owner

Correct Answer: E

QUESTION 134

Who should know the most about the progress toward a business objective or a release and be able to explain the alternatives most clearly?

A. The Project Manager.

B. The Product Owner.

C. The Scrum Master.

D. The Development Team.

Correct Answer: B

QUESTION 135

Which statement best describes a Product Owner's responsibility?

A. Manage the project and ensure the work meets the stakeholders' commitments.

B. Optimizing the Return on Investment (ROI) and the Total Cost of Ownership (TCO) of the work the Development Team does.

C. Keeping stakeholders at bay.

D. Directing the Development Team

Correct Answer: B

QUESTION 136

Who is on the Scrum Team?

A. The Scrum Master

B. The Product Owner

C. The Development Team

D. Project Manager

E. None of the above

Correct Answer: ABC

QUESTION 137

Which of the following are roles on a Scrum Team?

A. Product Owner

B. Scrum Master

C. Customers

D. Users

E. Development Team

Correct Answer: ABE

QUESTION 138

A Scrum Master keeps a list of open impediments, but it is growing, and they have been able to resolve only a small portion of the impediments. Which three techniques would be most helpful in this situation?

A. Arrange a triage meeting with all other project managers.

B. Alert management to the impediments and their impact.

C. Consult with the Development Team.

D. Tell the Product Owner that Scrum isn't working.

E. Prioritize the list and work on them in order.

F. Discuss the absence of management support with the Development Team.

Correct Answer: BCE

QUESTION 139

The reason the Scrum Master is at the Daily Scrum is:

A. Write down any changes to the Sprint Backlog, including adding new items and tracking progress on the burndown.

B. To make sure everyone answers the three questions in order of seniority.

C. They do not have to be there; they only have to ensure the Development Team has a Daily Scrum.

D. So they know what to report to management.

Correct Answer: C

QUESTION 140

Is Scrum Master is a "management" position?

A. True

B. False

Correct Answer: A

QUESTION 141

Which statement best describes the Sprint Review?

A. It is when the Scrum Team and stakeholders inspect the outcome of the Sprint and figure out what to do in the upcoming Sprint

B. It is a demo at the end of the Sprint for everyone in the organization to provide feedback on the work done.

C. It is a review of the team's activities during the Sprint.

D. It is used to congratulate the Development Team if it did what it committed to doing or to punish it if it failed to meet its commitments.

Correct Answer: A

QUESTION 142

The maximum length of the Sprint Review (its time box) is:

A. 1 day

B. 4 hours for a monthly Sprint, proportionally less for shorter Sprints

C. 2 hours

D. As long as needed

Correct Answer: B

Certification Sites

List of popular certification sites to become a Certified Scrum Master:

scrumalliance.org

1. Certified Scrum Master (CSM)

2. Advanced Certified Scrum Master (A-CSM)

scrum.org

1. Professional Scrum Master (PSM-I)

2. Professional Scrum Master II (PSM-II)

3. Professional Scrum Master III (PSM-III)

agileinstitute.com

1. Agile Institute (ACSM) -

2. Certified Agile Scrum Master (ACSM)

3. Advanced Certified Agile Scrum Master (A-ACSM)

pmi.org

Project Management Institute (PMI)

1. PMI Agile Certified Practitioner (PMI-ACP) -

iil.com

International Institute for Agile and Scrum (IIAS)

1. IIAS Certified Scrum Master (ICSM) -

Certified Scrum Master Prep Course

Realworldscrum.com

Other notable certifications

1. Certified Agile Practitioner (CAPM)

2. Agile Certified Manager (ACM)

3. Scrum Master Certification (SMC)

4. Certified Scrum Product Owner (CSPO)

Before choosing a certification, consider the following:

- **Cost**

- Course content

- Instructor Expertise

- Industry Recognition

- Continuing education requirements

Reference

- "Scrum: The Art of Doing Twice the Work in Half the Time" by Jeff Sutherland

- "Agile Project Management with Scrum" by Ken Schwaber

- "SMART Goals" by George T. Doran

- Scaledagile.com

- Silicon Valley 2014

Acronyms and Abbreviations used in Scrum and Agile

Comprehensive list of Scrum and Agile acronyms and abbreviations:

Scrum Framework

1. PO - Product Owner

2. SM - Scrum Master

3. Dev Team - Development Team

4. Sprint - Iterative development cycle

5. PBI - Product Backlog Item

6. INVEST - Independent, Negotiable, Valuable, Estimable, Small, Testable

7. DoD - Definition of Done

8. DoR - Definition of Ready

Agile Methodologies

1. XP - Extreme Programming

2. Kanban - Visual system for managing work

3. Lean - Lean Software Development

4. FDD - Feature-Driven Development

5. Crystal - Family of Agile methodologies

6. DSDM - Dynamic Systems Development Method

Roles and Responsibilities

1. PM - Project Manager

2. BA - Business Analyst

3. QA - Quality Assurance

4. Dev - Developer

5. UX - User Experience

6. UI - User Interface

Events and Ceremonies

1. SP - Sprint Planning

2. DS - Daily Scrum

3. SR - Sprint Review

4. SR - Sprint Retrospective

5. IPM - Iteration Planning Meeting

6. RPM - Release Planning Meeting

Artifacts

1. PB - Product Backlog

2. SB - Sprint Backlog

3. IB - Incremental Backlog

4. BRD - Business Requirements Document

5. FRD - Functional Requirements Document

Metrics and Measurements

1. BV - Business Value

2. PV - Priority Value

3. VP - Velocity Point

4. CPI - Cycle Performance Index

5. TPS - Team Performance Score

Other

1. MVP - Minimum Viable Product

2. MMF - Minimum Marketable Feature

3. KPI - Key Performance Indicator

4. ROI - Return on Investment

5. MoSCoW - Must-Haves, Should-Haves, Could-Haves, Won't-Haves